British Railways 'Britannia'

Alan C Butcher

Reviving the memories of yesterday…

ISBN 978-1-913251-33-8

First published in 2023 by Transport Treasury Publishing Ltd., 16 Highworth Close, High Wycombe, HP13 7PJ

www.ttpublishing.co.uk

Printed in Malta by Gutenberg Press Ltd., Tarxien, GXQ 2902

Front cover: No 70024 *Vulcan* on the sea wall at Teignmouth at the head of the 5.30am Paddington-Penzance express service on 19th July 1956. *RCR7732*

Frontispiece: No 70036 *Boadicea* is seen at Copper Mill junction, situated between Clapton and Tottenham Hale stations, on the London Liverpool Street-Cambridge line. *REV90B-6-1*

Above: No 70042 *Lord Roberts* on shed at its home depot of Willesden on 11th February 1962. *B. Wadey*

Opposite: Introduced in 1951, the 'Cornishman' was the name given to the 10.10am Penzance-Wolverhampton-Bradford service as evidenced by the large reporting number carried by No 70016 *Ariel. REV144-3*

Rear cover: No 70010 *Owen Glendower* on shed at Norwich Thorpe depot in company with No 70006 *Robert Burns. ICA BR160*

Contents

Introduction

The Transport Act of 1947 heralded the start of a new era on the railways as it created the British Transport Commission under which the railways, and road freight services, were taken into state ownership on 1st January 1948. Arrangements were well in hand before that date and the Railway Executive had appointed the various heads of department. The responsibility for locomotives and rolling stock was given to Robert Riddles who was designated Member for Electrical and Mechanical Engineering -otherwise known as Chief Mechanical Engineer.

With the new regime in charge, and the railways still suffering from the effects of World War 2, the way forward should have been either electrification or dieselisation. However the effects of the war and the relevant capital costs had to be taken into account, even today the cost of electrification is still an important consideration compared with the price of diesel traction. With electrification ruled out, dieselisation should have been the answer, but once again, the unit cost was high and fuel oil imported and paid for in US dollars that were in short supply. The answer was to continue with the construction of steam traction; this would keep the railways' own workshops in use and burn the fuel that was available below ground and supplies would last for centuries.

With the decision taken to continue with steam traction a series of Locomotive Exchanges between the newly formed Regions took place. One of the principal lessons learned was that large diameter driving wheels were not necessarily required to maintain high speeds, wide fireboxes would be required due to the deteriorating standard of coal available – the best was exported as the country required the foreign exchange to pay for imports. Working on steam locomotives is a filthy job and with improving living standards men were not willing to accept such conditions. For those that did join the footplate or maintenance departments the existence of National Service would result in a 'break of career'; not all would want to return to a 'dirty' job.

Stuart Cox was responsible for formulating proposals for the new Standard locomotives, the main considerations were:

- New designs were to be put forward whenever a step forward in reliability and efficiency could be realised
- Where an existing design offered a 'state of the art' approach only detailed modifications would be required
- The trend to be simplification, accessibility and reduction in time required for repairs and servicing.

Allied to this would be simplified shed preparation by means of grease and mechanical lubrication, wide traffic and route availability, allied with high steam raising capacity and bearing performance.

The last LMS-designed locomotives featured American practice with high running plates clear of the wheels, leaving them exposed to ease maintenance – which horrified the enthusiasts of the day. The first BR Standards followed this arrangement that initially did nothing to endear them to enthusiasts. However the drivers, and fitters, would appreciate that the need to crawl beneath the locomotive was much reduced.

Before production commenced a mock-up of the cab was produced and everyone who would have anything to do with the working of the locomotives, from inspector to drivers and firemen, were asked for their opinions with changes made following their suggestions – probably the first time they had been asked to comment on their working environment. Despite this there were several early complaints – draughty cabs, driver's position uncomfortably hot, fixed cab front windows. These were overcome, but the Standards to a certain extent suffered from the 'not invented here' syndrome which was common across the system, there were exceptions however. The locomotive crews on the Great Eastern main line – the destination for the first of the 'Britannia' class to enter traffic – took them to heart and they enabled the express services to be 'revolutionised'.

On 2nd January 1951, three years and one day after Nationalisation, No 70000 was steamed for the first time and underwent a series of trials in the north-west of England. On 30th January it was named Britannia by the then Transport Minister, the Right Honourable Alfred Barnes, at a ceremony at Marylebone station.

Despite the investment in the Standards, 999 in all, events dictated that the 'Britannia' class would have very short lives: the 'Britannia' first to go was No 70007 *Coeur-de-Lion* which was withdrawn from Carlisle Kingmoor in June 1965 – the last No 70013 *Oliver Cromwell*, which was the final steam locomotive to be overhauled at Crewe, lasted until the end of steam in August 1968. No 70050 *Firth of Clyde* was the shortest lived – 12 years and 2 days. But that was better than '9F' No 92220 *Evening Star*, at just 4 years, 11 months and 2 days.

Note on dates: The BR practice was to use the 'period ending' dates, using the Saturday as the end date. So unless the actual date is quoted then the dates recorded are either week ending, four ending; or in some cases five or six weeks ending.

Note for modellers: The new BR Standard Class 7 was anything but standard! As usual dated reference material is a must. Some of the more obvious differences include: tenders (see data panel for variations as built); front brake pipe hoses; lamp irons, Western Region allocations had 'end' on, others were 'side' on – which were changed when allocated to other regions – the Southern Region examples had additional ones on the smoke deflector support stays – and some were heightened; coupling rods – original fluted ones were replaced by rectangular ones (although some locomotives carried a mix of rods); sanding gear and height of filler lids on running boards; return crank – the original square pin or later four-stud design; footstep arrangement under the smokebox door; regulator operating rod support brackets; speedometer drive on left trailing axle; front cab windows – fixed or hinged; arrangement of draught excluders at rear of cab; and more obviously on the smoke deflectors the arrangement of the handrails which in most cases were replaced by handholds (of Western or London Midland Region-style) following an accident at Milton where it was claimed they obscured the view from the footplate.

Top: Still in primer, No 70023 stands outside Crewe Works on 9th August 1951 waiting to be connected to its tender before being taken into the Paint Shop to be decorated in BR's Brunswick Green livery lined in black and orange. With smartly dressed observers present perhaps the locomotive has just been named as the plates are fitted. One wonders if the painters then removed them before applying paint to the smoke deflectors. The locomotive was accepted into traffic on the 21st August, being allocated to Old Oak Common at the end of the month.

Bottom: Smartly dressed and ready to roll, No 70015 *Apollo* stands outside Crewe Works. The image is undated but as the original step arrangement below the smokebox and fluted coupling rods are in evidence it may well be when new to traffic on 12th June 1951 and no shed plate is fitted. Initially allocated to Camden it moved to the Great Eastern section in May 1952 before heading to the Western Region in September 1953.

No	Name	To Traffic	Tender	First shed	Allocation 7/62	Last shed	Withdrawn
70000	Britannia	05/01/1951	BR1	Stratford	Norwich Thorpe	Newton Heath	28/05/1966
70001	Lord Hurcomb	14/02/1951	BR1	Stratford	March	Carlisle Kingmoor	03/09/1966
70002	Geoffrey Chaucer	06/03/1951	BR1	Stratford	March	Carlisle Kingmoor	14/01/1967
70003	John Bunyan	01/03/1951	BR1	Stratford	March	Carlisle Kingmoor	25/03/1967
70004	William Shakespeare	30/03/1951	BR1	Stratford	Willesden	Carlisle Kingmoor	30/12/1967
70005	John Milton	07/04/1951	BR1	Stratford	March	Carlisle Kingmoor	29/07/1967
70006	Robert Burns	12/04/1951	BR1	Stratford	March	Carlisle Kingmoor	20/05/1967
70007	Coeur-de-Lion	25/04/1951	BR1	Stratford	March	Carlisle Kingmoor	19/06/1965
70008	Black Prince	28/04/1951	BR1	Norwich Thorpe	March	Carlisle Kingmoor	14/01/1967
70009	Alfred the Great	04/05/1951	BR1	Norwich Thorpe	March	Carlisle Kingmoor	21/01/1967
70010	Owen Glendower	05/05/1951	BR1	Norwich Thorpe	March	Carlisle Kingmoor	23/09/1967
70011	Hotspur	14/05/1951	BR1	Norwich Thorpe	March	Carlisle Kingmoor	23/12/1967
70012	John of Gaunt	21/05/1951	BR1	Norwich Thorpe	March	Carlisle Kingmoor	30/12/1967
70013	Oliver Cromwell	30/05/1951	BR1	Norwich Thorpe	March	Carnforth	17/08/1968
70014	Iron Duke	02/06/1951	BR1	Nine Elms	Annesley	Carlisle Kingmoor	30/12/1967
70015	Apollo	12/06/1951	BR1	Camden	Annesley	Carlisle Kingmoor	05/08/1967
70016	Ariel	18/06/1951	BR1	Holbeck	Longsight	Carlisle Kingmoor	19/08/1967
70017	Arrow	02/06/1951	BR1	Old Oak Common	Aston	Carlisle Kingmoor	01/10/1966
70018	Flying Dutchman	25/06/1951	BR1	Old Oak Common	Longsight	Carlisle Kingmoor	24/12/1966
70019	Lightning	30/06/1951	BR1	Newton Abbot	Longsight	Carlisle Upperby	12/03/1966
70020	Mercury	31/07/1951	BR1	Old Oak Common	Longsight	Carlisle Kingmoor	21/01/1967
70021	Morning Star	03/08/1951	BR1	Laira	Willesden	Carlisle Kingmoor	30/12/1967
70022	Tornado	16/08/1951	BR1	Laira	Longsight	Carlisle Kingmoor	23/12/1967
70023	Venus	21/08/1951	BR1	Old Oak Common	Longsight	Carlisle Kingmoor	30/12/1967
70024	Vulcan	06/10/1951	BR1	Laira	Aston	Carlisle Kingmoor	30/12/1967
70025	Western Star	13/09/1952	BR1A	Cardiff Canton	Aston	Carlisle Kingmoor	23/12/1967
70026	Polar Star	07/10/1952	BR1A	Cardiff Canton	Aston	Stockport Edgeley	14/01/1967
70027	Rising Star	24/10/1952	BR1A	Cardiff Canton	Aston	Carlisle Kingmoor	01/07/1967
70028	Royal Star	27/10/1952	BR1A	Cardiff Canton	Longsight	Carlisle Kingmoor	16/09/1967
70029	Shooting Star	08/11/1952	BR1A	Cardiff Canton	Aston	Carlisle Kingmoor	21/10/1967
70030	William Wordsworth	19/11/1952	BR1	Holyhead	March	Carlisle Upperby	25/06/1966
70031	Byron	29/11/1952	BR1	Holyhead	Aston	Carlisle Kingmoor	11/11/1967
70032	Tennyson	10/12/1952	BR1	Holyhead	Willesden	Carlisle Kingmoor	30/09/1967
70033	Charles Dickens	13/12/1952	BR1	Holyhead	Willesden	Carlisle Kingmoor	15/07/1967
70034	Thomas Hardy	20/12/1952	BR1	Longsight	March	Carlisle Kingmoor	06/05/1967
70035	Rudyard Kipling	22/12/1952	BR1	Norwich Thorpe	Immingham	Carlisle Kingmoor	30/12/1967
70036	Boadicea	23/12/1952	BR1	Stratford	Immingham	Carlisle Kingmoor	15/10/1966
70037	Hereward the Wake	24/12/1952	BR1	Stratford	Immingham	Carlisle Kingmoor	05/11/1966
70038	Robin Hood	29/01/1953	BR1	Stratford	Immingham	Carlisle Kingmoor	12/08/1967
70039	Sir Christopher Wren	09/02/1953	BR1	Norwich Thorpe	Immingham	Carlisle Kingmoor	23/09/1967
70040	Clive of India	21/03/1953	BR1	Norwich Thorpe	Immingham	Carlisle Kingmoor	15/04/1967
70041	Sir John Moore	20/03/1953	BR1	Stratford	Immingham	Carlisle Kingmoor	15/04/1967
70042	Lord Roberts	09/04/1953	BR1	Stratford	Willesden	Carlisle Kingmoor	13/05/1967
70043	Lord Kitchener	04/06/1953	BR1	Longsight	Aston	Crewe South	07/08/1965
70044	Earl Haig	04/06/1953	BR1	Longsight	Holbeck	Stockport Edgeley	24/10/1966
70045	Lord Rowallan	14/06/1953	BR1D	Holyhead	Aston	Carlisle Kingmoor	31/12/1967
70046	Anzac	22/06/1953	BR1D	Holyhead	Aston	Carlisle Kingmoor	08/07/1967
70047	—	25/06/1954	BR1D	Holyhead	Aston	Carlisle Kingmoor	29/07/1967
70048	The Territorial Army, 1908-1958	08/07/1954	BR1D	Holyhead	Annesley	Carlisle Kingmoor	06/05/1967
70049	Solway Firth	28/07/1954	BR1D	Holyhead	Annesley	Carlisle Kingmoor	09/12/1967
70050	Firth of Clyde	04/08/1954	BR1D	Polmadie	Corkerhill	Carlisle Kingmoor	06/08/1966
70051	Firth of Forth	11/08/1954	BR1D	Polmadie	Corkerhill	Carlisle Kingmoor	16/12/1967
70052	Firth of Tay	21/08/1954	BR1D	Polmadie	Corkerhill	Carlisle Kingmoor	01/04/1967
70053	Moray Firth	03/09/1954	BR1D	Polmadie	Holbeck	Carlisle Kingmoor	15/04/1967
70054	Dornoch Firth	13/09/1954	BR1D	Polmadie	Holbeck	Carlisle Kingmoor	26/11/1966

Class Data

Introduced: 1951

Driving wheel diameter: 6ft 2in

Boiler pressure: 250 psi

Cylinders (2): 20in x 28in

Nominal tractive effort: 32,105 lb

Locomotive weight in working order: 94 tons
Bogie – 17 tons 2cwt
Drivers – 20 tons 5cwt
Trailing truck – 16 tons 3cwt

Tenders: BR1 – coal capacity: 7 tons, water capacity 4,250gal; weight 49 tons 3cwt
BR1A – coal capacity: 7 tons, water capacity 5,000gal; weight 49 tons 10cwt
BR1D – coal capacity: 9 tons, water capacity 4,750gal; weight 54 tons 10cwt (those fitted to No 70050-54 were fitted with coal pushers).

Boilers: length between tube plates – 17ft; firebox external length – 7ft; tubes 40 large @ 5½in OD, 136 small @ 2 1/8 in; superheater elements 18.

Length: wheelbase 58ft 3in; over buffers 68ft 9in.

Bibliography and Further Reading

Bond, Roland C., *A Lifetime with Locomotives*, Goose & Son Publishers, 0900404302, 1975.
Cornwell, E. L., (Ed), *Locomotives Illustrated: 10 – BR Standard Pacifics*, Ian Allan, 1977.
Cox, E. S., *British Railways Standard Steam Locomotives*, Ian Allan, no ISBN, 1966.
Derry, R., *The Book of the Britannia Pacifics,* Irwell Press, 9781903266489, 2004.
Griffiths, R. & Smith, P.; *The Directory of British Engine Sheds and Principal Locomotive Servicing Points: Vol 1,* 9780860935421, OPC, 1999.
Griffiths, R. & Smith, P.; *The Directory of British Engine Sheds and Principal Locomotive Servicing Points: Vol 2,* 9780860935483, OPC, 2000.
Grindlay, Jim, *British Railways Steam Locomotive Allocations 1948-1968: Part 5 BR Standard & Ex-War Department 70000-92250*, Modelmaster Publications, 9780954426253, 2006.
Haresnape, B., *Ivatt & Riddles Locomotives: A Pictorial History*, Ian Allan, 0711007950, 1977.
Longworth, H.; *British Railways Steam Locomotives 1948-1968*, 9780860935933, OPC, 2005.
Longworth, H.; *British Railways Steam Locomotive Allocations*, 9780860936428, OPC, 2011.
RCTS, *A Detailed History of British Railways Standard Steam Locomotives: Vol 1 – Background to Standardisation and the Pacific Classes*, RCTS, 0901115819, 1994.
Swinger, P., *BR Standard Pacifics in Colour*, Ian Allan, 978071102264X, 1994.
Walmsley, T., *Shed by Shed, Part One, London Midland,* 9780956061553, 2010.
Walmsley, T., *Shed by Shed, Part Two, Eastern,* 9780956061560, 2010.
Walmsley, T., *Shed by Shed, Part Four, Scottish*, 9780956061577, 2011.
Walmsley, T., *Shed by Shed, Part Six, Western*, 9780956061522, 2009.
Whiteley, J. S., & Morrison, G. W., *The Power of the BR Standard Pacifics*, OPC, 086093067X, 1980.
Williams, Alan, *BR Standard Steam Album*, Ian Allan, 0711010102, 1980.
–, *abc British Railways Locomotives: Combined Volume*, Winter 1955/56, Ian Allan, 9780711005068, reprinted 1999.
–, *abc British Railways Locomotives: Combined Volume*, Summer 1957, Ian Allan, 9780711038455, reprinted 2016.
–, *abc British Railways Locomotives: Combined Volume*, Summer 1958, Ian Allan, 9780711037694, reprinted 2013.

The following websites were useful in confirming data, rail tour information, etc:
www.brdatabase.info
www.gracesguide.co.uk
www.sixbellsjunction.co.uk
www.shipsnostalgia.com

Chapter 1 - On the Great Eastern

Above: No 70005 *John Milton* was delivered to Stratford depot on 7th April 1951 and is seen on the turntable at London Liverpool Street. This table was operated using a vacuum-powered motor using the locomotive's braking system, the cylinder alongside the deck provided a reservoir should the need arise. Situated between the Primrose Street and Pindar Street over-bridges, it enabled locomotives to be turned without the need to visit Stratford depot, speeding up turn-round time between services. The facility became redundant on 9th September 1962 with dieselisation of the area. At the time of the photograph No 70005 was allocated to Norwich and shows that the step below the smokebox has been modified, compare with No 70006 opposite; the tender carries the second version of the BR emblem introduced in 1956. *NS207644*

Opposite top: No 70006 *Robert Burns* awaits departure from Liverpool Street with an express service very soon after delivery on 12th April 1951 as it carries a Stratford shed plate; it moved to Norwich a few weeks later in early May. It returned to Stratford in October (including a period in store) before a return to Norwich in November where it stayed for the next 10 years. It already has the modified rectangular section connecting rods between the first and second coupled wheel sets. In an adjacent platform LNER Class B12/3 No 61557 was built for the Great Eastern Railway by William Beardmore Ltd in February 1921 and had a service life of almost 36 years, by comparison the 'Britannia' lasted just over 16. The sloping top edge of the tender tank was a hazard for those involved when watering and was soon modified with a horizontal foot step. The first 25 locomotives were soon modified, although as usual a few took a little longer to be modified.

Opposite bottom: No 70030 *William Wordsworth* was delivered to Holyhead depot on 19th November 1952, and reallocated to Longsight the following month. A move to Dover came in May 1953 when the Southern Region Bulleid Pacifics were temporarily withdrawn for suspected axle-flaws. Returning to Longsight, it originally arrived at Norwich in June 1953, moving to Yarmouth South Town in September 1958 and back to Norwich in January 1959. It is seen on 2nd October 1958 at London Liverpool Street, still carrying the additional SR lamp brackets as a reminder of its stint at Dover. The smoke deflectors carry the LMR-style handholds and additional handrail. *RCR12837*

70006
70030
WILLIAM WORDSWORTH
70030

Above: Following its journey Up to London, No 70039 *Sir Christopher Wren* runs into Liverpool Street on 4th May 1956 at the head of the 'East Anglian', in doing so it passes classmate No 70040 Clive of India waiting to take a service into East Anglia. No 70039 entered traffic on 9th February 1953 when it was allocated to Norwich, it moved to Stratford in June where it would spend almost the next six years before a return to Norwich. *RCR5919*

Below: Minutes after leaving London Liverpool Street en route for Norwich No 70039 *Sir Christopher Wren* is seen at Bishopsgate, behind the building on the right was Bishopsgate Goods Yard – the main location for rail freight arriving from the eastern counties in central London. The platform on the left was not part of the Low Level station here, which is hidden by an Up service. No 70039 had acquired the LMR-style handholds on the deflectors by July 1959, probably during a General Overhaul at Doncaster earlier that year. *REV124-3*

No 70011 *Hotspur* is seen at Bethnal Green with an Up express on 16th February 1957. Delivered on 14th May 1951 this was one of seven locomotives that experienced wheels moving on the axles. No 70011's occurred at Hatfield Peverel on 4th September 1951 whilst working an early morning newspaper train. A cure was found and rectified during a visit to Crewe Works between 9th September and 29th November 1951. The branding 'Starcraft', was the trade name of S. Spanglett Ltd, 20-24 St Mathews Row, Bethnal Green Road, manufacturers of furniture, including radiograms built into cocktail cabinets. *RCR10196*

THE
ESSEX COAST
EXPRESS
70013

Opposite Top: On Friday 31st July 1959 No 70013 *Oliver Cromwell* heads to the seaside as it passes through Bethnal Green with the Down 'Essex Coast Express' that ran from London Liverpool Street to Clacton from 1958 to 1968. The state of the locomotive leaves a bit to be desired considering it emerged from Doncaster Works following a General Overhaul as recently as 9th May. By now it sports the LMR-style handholds on the deflectors, along with additional short horizontal handles, and AWS cover plate beneath the buffer beam. Allocated new to Norwich, on 30th May 1951, its final allocation on the Great Eastern was to March in September 1961, before the usual move to the LMR. Destined for preservation, it was noted on 16th February 1968 as being sheeted over at Carnforth shed. *PP1093*

Opposite Bottom: Following its introduction to service on 21st March 1953 No 70040 *Clive of India* was initially allocated to Norwich, moving to Stratford a few weeks later. It is seen here as it heads a Down express through Bethnal Green on 16th February 1957. From this locomotive onwards the trailing truck had plain bearings, with different covers to the previous Timken fitted examples. The train consists of pre-Nationalisation coaching stock, with the majority in 'blood and custard' colours. *RCR10197*

Right: On 22nd September 1956 No 70012 *John of Gaunt* is illustrated on shed at Stratford with the fireman raking out the remnants of the fire, having used the rocking grate facility to clean the fire by breaking up any clinker and shake ash into the pan. The design used on the 'Britannias' was based on that used on the Southern's 'Merchant Navy' class Pacifics. Allocated new to Norwich on 14th May 1951, a move to Stratford came in November 1958. It had a short 'holiday' at Yarmouth South Town in early 1959 before moving west to Norwich where it would remain until moving to March in September 1961. *AEB1797*

THE
HOOK
CONTINENTAL
70034
THOMAS HARDY
70034

70036

Opposite Top: At its home depot, No 70034 *Thomas Hardy* is pictured sporting the 'Hook Continental' headboard at Stratford on 18th May 1957. The named train commenced operation between London and Harwich's Parkeston Quay in 1929, and except for a break during World War 2 ran until 1987. No 70034 entered traffic on 20th December 1952 initially at Longsight before a move to the Southern Region at Stewarts Lane where it acquired the additional lamp irons on the smoke deflector stays. Returning to Longsight in June 1953, transfer to Stratford occurred the following month.

Opposite Bottom: No 70036 *Boadicea* entered traffic on 23rd December 1952 and is seen on shed at Stratford in September 1957 which was its home until transfer to Norwich in January 1959. Nineteen members of the 55 strong class were allocated to Stratford from the introduction of No 70000 in January 1951 until January 1959 when the remaining examples were transferred away, many going to Norwich, as Stratford depot was to be reconfigured for the new era. By January 1963 the depot had a sole steam locomotive ('B1' No 61144) on its books along with numerous diesel shunters and main line locomotives. Today the site is occupied by Stratford International station and the Westfield Stratford City shopping centre.

Below: Bulled to perfection, No 70037 *Hereward the Wake* is seen on shed at Stratford complete with the 'Day Continental' headboard. Note that all three of the buffer beam lamp irons have been heightened. The shunter off to the right No 11505, dates the image to some time between February 1956, its date of introduction and July 1961 when it was renumbered D2955; it survived until February 1962. No 70037 underwent a General Overhaul at Crewe between 17th February and 29th March 1956 and the modified step was acquired between 9th and 13th April so is probably seen soon after its return to Stratford. *REV230-1*

No 70001 *Lord Hurcomb* on an Up express passenger service alongside the Ilford flyover on 21st April 1951. Delivery had been to Stratford depot only a matter of weeks before, entering traffic on 14th February – it had been named at Crewe on 6th February. In the 1930s the flyover had been constructed just west of Ilford to switch the main and electric lines over, to enable main line trains to utilise Liverpool Street's longer west side platforms without having to cross east side suburban traffic in the station throat. The suburban lines from Liverpool Street to Shenfield were electrified at 1,500V dc and work was started on implementing this. However, the outbreak of World War 2 brought the project to a temporary halt and it was not until 1949 that the scheme was completed with electrification being extended to Chelmsford in 1956. *REV53B-1-2*

No 70005 *John Milton* is seen climbing Brentwood Bank bound for Harwich during the time it was allocated to Stratford. The 'Day Continental' was a boat train that ran from London Liverpool Street to Harwich Parkeston Quay enabling passengers to travel across the North Sea to the Hook of Holland. In 1955 the Harwich-Hook services were run by turbine steamers Arnhem (1947, 4,891grt) and Amsterdam (1950, 5,092grt) owned by British Railways. S. M. Zeeland operated the *Koningin Emma* and *Princess Beatrix* (both 1939, 4,353grt). The BR vessels with extensive berthing accommodation operated the overnight service whilst the SMZ vessels had a much larger passenger certificate for day operation. *NS207649*

No 70036 *Boadicea* is seen near Ingrave, between Brentwood & Warley and Shenfield & Hutton stations, on 2nd August 1954. Initially double track, the section of line between Gidea Park and Shenfield was quadrupled in 1934 to cater for increased traffic with overhead electrification following for suburban traffic. Despite the new motive power, the customer continued to be carried in pre-Nationalisation carriages, albeit painted in BR's 'blood & custard' livery.

Above: No 70010 *Owen Glendower* has charge of the 1.30pm Liverpool Street to Cromer service near Shenfield on 11th April 1953. Introduced into traffic on 5th May 1951 and allocated to Norwich, the locomotive spent the next 10 years at the shed. No 70010 would take the train to Norwich where, with a locomotive swap, the train would reverse and complete the journey to the coast. The locomotive would not receive the front step modification until a visit to Crewe for a Heavy Intermediate overhaul in spring 1956.

Below: No 70016 *Ariel* takes the 'Norfolkman' northwards from Shenfield during 1952. Delivered on 18th June 1951, it was allocated to Leeds Holbeck (albeit on loan from the Western Region). Transfer to Stratford occurred in March 1952, before returning to the Western Region at Laira depot in July 1953. The overhead gantries in the background were as far as the 1,500V dc electrification had reached in 1949 with the extension completed to Southend in 1956. The conversion to the, by now standard, 25kV would not take place on the Southend route until 1979. *NS207813*

Above: No 70037 *Hereward the Wake* is seen climbing Ingrave bank near Ingatestone on 1st September 1955 whilst working a Royal train for HRH King Frederick of Denmark. Returning home, on 9th September, the King, accompanied by Queen Ingrid, opened the British Trade Fair in Copenhagen's Tivoli Gardens. In November 1960 No 70037 left Norwich for March depot before transferring to Immingham in October 1961. Note the heightened lamp irons on the buffer beam and the first version of the modified front step beneath the smokebox. *REV99-4*

Below: No 70034 *Thomas Hardy* has charge of a Parkeston Quay-London Liverpool Street service at Ingatestone on 16th September 1956. It would remain at Stratford until a move to Norwich in January 1959, before moving to March depot in June 1961. Of interest is the number of cross-arms on the lineside telegraph poles – with today's signalling systems the pole routes are part of the railway of history; incidentally the pole routes typically used 200lb (per mile) copper wire, more for mechanical strength than conductivity. *B. Wadey*

Above: Having passed over Witham junction, No 70036 *Boadicea* runs into the station with a southbound service on 21st November 1959. As the station running in board suggests this was the junction for the two branches. Off to the west ran the line to Bishop's Stortford via Braintree, while the line to Maldon East & Heybridge exited to the east. Passenger services to Maldon ceased on 7th September 1964 with total closure in April 1966 when freight services ceased. No 70036 has the final arrangement of front step. *AEB5193*

Below: No 70012 *John of Gaunt* has passed through Witham with a northbound service on 10th May 1958 basically still in as-built condition. The firm of Hugh Baird & Sons Ltd dates from 1823 and is still in business at Witham today where it operates one of its two pneumatic malting plants as Bairds Malt. The line leading off to the right was the line to Bishop's Stortford, which today terminates at Braintree – the through route closing to passengers on 3rd March 1952. *RCR11804*

Above: No 70002 *Geoffrey Chaucer* at the head of an Up express at Kelvedon on 6th April 1957. This was the junction for the Kelvedon & Tollesbury Light Railway which was authorised under the Light Railways Act 1896 and operated between the two villages of Kelvedon (on the Great Eastern main line) and Tollesbury to the south of Colchester on the coast. The line, authorised on 29th January 1901, was opened on 1st October 1904. Closure to passenger traffic took place on 5th May 1951, freight traffic continued between Tollesbury Pier and Tiptree until 29th October of the same year. The section between Tiptree and Kelvedon continued in use for freight traffic until 28th September 1962. Tiptree is still the home of the jam-making firm of Wilkes & Sons, founded in 1885, which provided a large amount of freight traffic. The locomotive sports heightened lamp brackets above the buffers, showing an interesting variation to the express passenger head code. *RCR10395*

Below: Delivered from Crewe Works on 9th April 1953, three years later on 6th October 1956 No 70042 *Lord Roberts* powers the 12.45 Up service from Norwich towards Marks Tey station; passing a diesel multiple unit in the loop and a steam locomotive in the yard. This was where the Marks Tey, Sudbury & Bury branch (otherwise known as the Stour Valley line) left the main line; the line to Sudbury remains open. The line leading off sharply to the left once served a turntable. *RCR10062*

Delivered new to Norwich depot on 22nd December 1952, No 70035 *Rudyard Kipling* is seen at Colchester on 14th August the following year on its way to Norwich. Sitting outside the shed (to the right of the image) is Class J15 No 65448, dating from 1899. No 70035 was transferred away from Great Eastern metals in September 1961 when it was transferred to Immingham. Today, with the unusual layout of platforms, Colchester station has the longest physical platform in the UK as the entire length (from platform 3 to 4) measures 620m (2,034ft); however Gloucester has the longest unbroken platform at 1,977ft.

New to traffic on 20th March 1953, No 70041 *Sir John Moore* runs an Up express service through Colchester during the time it was allocated to Norwich depot; it had arrived from Stratford during January 1959. The white diamond on the signal post indicates that the area is track circuited and that the train crew need not contact the signalman if held at a signal for an undue length of time. Note that whilst the Clacton/Walton-on-the-Naze branch has been electrified, the main lines will not be electrified for several years. *NS207636*

The Summer 1950 timetable saw the introduction of a regular interval service between Liverpool Street and Clacton, which left Liverpool Street on the half-hour and Clacton on the hour. January 1951 saw the introduction of the 'Britannia' class, along with a speeding up of services on the Great Eastern line. No 70005 *John Milton* is seen at Thorpe-le-Soken on 17th June 1958; as can be seen the encroachment of the overhead is taking place. Soon steam will be replaced by electric multiple units, with Clacton first seeing electric trains on 16th March 1959. Initially, the line was only electrified as far as Colchester, with through electrified services to Liverpool Street commencing on 7th January 1963. *PH000284*

Flying the flag as the first of the 999 BR Standards was No 70000 *Britannia*, it is seen on 9th June 1956 just to the north of Bentley Junction – to the south of Ipswich – at the head of an express passenger service bound for London Liverpool Street. The left hand line, signalled for reversible working, served the Hadleigh branch, there being no connection to the main line at the point of divergence. No 70000's first depot was Stratford where it stayed until January 1959 when it relocated to Norwich. An early indication that all might not be well with the new design was the fact that within less than 18 months of introduction it had fractured its mainframe. *RCR7357*

Top: One necessity for a steam locomotive was a supply of water and the ability to take on supplies whilst on the move. No 70011 *Hotspur* demonstrates its ability to take on water as it passes over the troughs to the south of Halifax junction near Ipswich. No 70011 spent its first 10 years allocated to Norwich before a transfer to March depot in September 1961, where it was noted as being stored in early 1963 as diesels began to take over in East Anglia. Transfer to the LMR took place at the end of 1963 when it was reallocated to Carlisle Kingmoor. *REV223-2*

Bottom: No 70040 *Clive of India* is seen at Halifax junction just to the south of Ipswich, during the time it was allocated to Stratford – the modified front step had been acquired by December 1956. Halifax junction is where the current route diverges from the line that went to the original Eastern Union Railway station in Ipswich that closed on 1st July 1860. The right hand line leads to Griffen Wharf on the River Orwell. Following its second stint at Norwich, No 70040 was relocated to Immingham at the end of 1960. *REV223-3*

Below: The fireman takes a break as No 70009 *Alfred the Great* runs into Ipswich station at the head of a stopping passenger service. Delivered new from Crewe on 4th May 1951, the locomotive was reallocated to Nine Elms a matter of weeks later and is seen following its return to the Great Eastern section in October 1951. The locomotive is not carrying a shed plate so this picture was probably taken soon after its return to Norwich depot following its stint on the Southern Region as it has the additional lamp irons on the smoke deflector stays.

Bottom: Right: No 70036 *Boadicea* runs into Ipswich with a southbound service on 10th August 1953. For the fastest London Liverpool Street-Norwich services this was the one and only station stop. The schedule allowed 73 minutes for the 68.7 miles to Ipswich and, after a two-minute station stop, 45 minutes were allowed for the 46.3 mile run to Norwich. The number of sacks on the platform is a reminder that at one time the railways carried all of the long-distance mail. Initially allocated to Stratford, the locomotive was transferred to Norwich in January 1959. It moved to March in November 1960 then to Immingham in September 1961 before a transfer to the LMR in November 1963. Withdrawal from Kingmoor came on 15th October 1966.

The 'Broadsman' enters Ipswich station behind No 70007 *Coeur-de-Lion* on 28th May 1953. Being only a matter of days before the Coronation of Queen Elizabeth II at Westminster Abbey, the locomotive is carrying an additional headboard to commemorate the event. The 'Broadsman' ran between London Liverpool Street and Cromer/Sheringham from 1950 until 1962; a locomotive change would take place at Norwich as the class was banned from running north of the city due to its axle-loading weight. New to Stratford on 25th April 1951, No 70007 would transfer to its final depot of Carlisle Kingmoor, via Norwich (from May 1951) and March (from November 1961), in December 1963. It was the first member of the class to be withdrawn on 19th June 1965, and would be the only example to be broken up at Crewe Works during July, almost as if BR wanted to destroy the evidence it had existed as quickly as possible having survived in traffic for 14 years, 1 month and 25 days. *REV74B-5-3*

Above: No 70038 *Robin Hood* pulls into Ipswich on 10th August 1953, seven months into its six-year stay at Stratford depot, at the head of the 'East Anglian' express service that first ran in 1937. The carriages have been repainted into BR Crimson Lake and Cream livery and are complete with train name-boards. Delivered to Stratford on 29th January 1953, No 70038 was transferred to Norwich in January 1959, moving to March depot in November 1960, then onto Immingham in October 1961 following a General Overhaul at Doncaster between 12th August and 20th October when it was fitted with BR's Automatic Warning System.

Below: No 70013 *Oliver Cromwell* and former London, Tilbury & Southend Railway Class 79 No 80 Thundersley (BR No 41966) stand at Diss awaiting transfer to Alan Bloom's Bressingham Steam Museum in August 1968. No 70013 had run the Manchester Victoria-Carlisle section of the 'Fifteen Guinea Special' marking the end of standard gauge steam on BR on 11th August 1968 before running light engine to Diss. The nameplates had been removed for the trip with its name painted on the smoke deflectors. Withdrawal occurred on 17th August as otherwise BR would have broken its own steam ban! Final transfer to Bressingham would be by road. *BR197*

Above: No 70041 *Sir John Moore* heads a southbound service beneath the over-bridge at Hartford on 11th September 1954. This was where the Norfolk Railway's Wymondham-Norwich line passed beneath the Eastern Union's Tivetshall-Norwich line. The appearance of the locomotive leaves a little to be desired, although a visit to Crewe Works for a Light Intermediate overhaul the following November would improve its looks. *REV86A-1-5*

Below: A couple of miles to the north the two routes met at Trowse Lower junction, one mile from Norwich according to the sign on the signal box. No 70041 takes its train past the cattle docks. With the demise of steam the sidings here were used to store withdrawn locomotives destined for King & Son's Norwich scrapyard – although no 'Britannias' were to meet their end here, several of Sir Nigel Gresley's 'A3' racehorses did, along with locomotives from the Southern and Western regions. With only a short distance to journey's end the fireman is taking it easy.

No 70001 *Lord Hurcomb* crosses Trowse swing-bridge just outside Norwich station, taking an express south to London Liverpool Street. The locomotive spent almost eight years allocated to Stratford before transferring to Norwich in January 1959. The bridge, originally built in 1845 by George Parker Bidder, was rebuilt in 1905 and again in 1987. The 1905 bridge is seen here with a single red flag flying, indicating that the bridge is operational. *REV102-4*

70002

RCTS
70003
JOHN BUNYAN

Opposite Top: Nearing the end of its journey from London, No 70002 *Geoffrey Chaucer* approaches Trowse swing-bridge over the River Yare on 11th August 1953 passing the cattle docks as it does so. A few yards in front of the locomotive are the approaches to the well-known Carrow Works factory complex, the earliest part of which was built in 1856 by the Colman family (the site was previously known as Paper Mill Yard). To the left is Class B1 No 61360, built by NBL in May 1950, standing in the sidings to the east of the running lines.

Opposite Bottom: On 31st March 1962 the RCTS ran the 'Great Eastern Commemorative Steam Rail Tour' from London Liverpool Street headed by No 70003 *John Bunyan*. With Norwich as the initial destination the train visited the former Victoria station (by now a goods depot) and during the 20-minute layover at Victoria participants were allowed to alight from the carriages using portable steps. The train then returned to Trowse Upper junction before taking the line to Thorpe station. A trip over the remaining lines via Dereham to Foulsham and Swaffham behind Class J15 No 65567 ended at Thetford where the 'Britannia' took over for the journey back to London. Following servicing at Norwich depot, No 70003 ran light engine to Thetford to take over from the 'J15' for the trip back to London (see page 40). By the date of the trip No 70003 was allocated to March depot, moving to Carlisle Kingmoor on 1st December 1963.

Above: A somewhat work-stained No 70005 *John Milton* enters Norwich as it passes over Thorpe junction in May 1955, having passed under the over-bridge that carries Carrow Road over the line. The locomotive was shedded at Stratford at the time, before relocating to Norwich in January 1959 and then to March depot in September 1961. In February 1963 No 70005 was noted as being stored at March depot having been replaced on East Anglian services by Type 3 diesels. Transferred to the LMR at Willesden by the end of March, it was then transferred to Aston then onto Carlisle Kingmoor by October 1964. *REV242-3*

Above: No 70006 *Robert Burns* passes Trowse Upper Junction box on its way to London Liverpool Street on 11th August 1957. It now carries a complete set of rectangular section connecting rods. The sign in front of the telegraph pole indicates the speed limit, 40mph, across the junction in the direction of the arrow that was the main line into Norwich Thorpe station. The line straight ahead led to the site of the town's Victoria station that closed to passengers on 22nd May 1916 but remained in use as a general goods depot until 31st January 1966; it continued in use as a coal concentration depot until September 1986.

Below: No 70009 *Alfred the Great* rolls into Norwich on 15th August 1953 at the head of the 'Broadsman' express service from Liverpool Street. With another locomotive attached to the rear of the train it would continue its journey through the Norfolk countryside to Cromer and Sheringham, leaving the original locomotive to be serviced on Norwich shed. No 70009 would leave Norwich for March depot in September 1961. In February 1962 it was reported that: '*Britannias* 70000/1/2/3/5/6-13 were all placed in store at March in February due to further dieselisation by Type 3 diesels from Darnall and these now cover several March freight turns; three of the Britannias are understood to be unserviceable due to frost damage'. The elderly looking carriage to the left is a former North Eastern Railway Third, No E52108E, dating from March 1914, and withdrawn in 1953.

The driver has a quick look over No 70010 *Owen Glendower* as it waits for departure time from Norwich bound for Liverpool Street. Compared with the previous image, on page 18, the locomotive has gained a modified front step (in April 1956) and additional handrail on the smoke deflectors in line with the running board – the original handrails having been replaced by LMR-style handholds. Allocated to Norwich from new, No 70010 would remain there until transferred to March in December 1961, followed by the usual relocation to the LMR – at Willesden – on 30th March 1963. *WS277*

Above: No 70030 *William Wordsworth* passes the Permanent Way yards on the approach to Norwich during May 1955 during its first stint allocated to the nearby depot. When the image is enlarged, it can be seen that the guard's carriage door is open with him looking out, so one wonders if the shot was pre-planned. The extensive sidings, conveniently hidden behind the locomotive, are now the site of Crown Point Traction Maintenance Depot opened on 27th October 1982, by the chairman of the British Railways Board, Peter Parker. It replaced Norwich engine shed and allowed InterCity trains that had been serviced at Great Yarmouth to move to a central location. It was electrified in 1985, along with the Great Eastern main line. *REV233-2*

Opposite Top: No 70034 *Thomas Hardy* waits for the road to the adjacent depot while 70039 *Sir Christopher Wren* rolls into Norwich with the 'Norfolkman', the London Liverpool Street-Sheringham service. The named train, which operated from 1947 until 1962, will need to reverse at the terminus, and, together with a change of motive power, to continue its journey to the north Norfolk coast. 'Britannias' were not used north of Norwich and it was not until the preservation era that No 70013 *Oliver Cromwell* visited the North Norfolk Railway, at Sheringham, and worked north of the city.

Opposite Bottom: No 70030 *William Wordsworth* heads south through Saxmundham station on 5th August 1959, whilst working a Norwich-London Liverpool Street service. Just to the north of the station the branch to Aldeburgh left the main line and although truncated remains to serve the nearby Sizewell nuclear power stations. No 70030 left the Eastern Region in July 1963 when it was reallocated to Crewe (North). It was the only 'Britannia' to be withdrawn from Carlisle Upperby depot, on 25th June 1966, and stored at Wigan Springs Branch before being consigned to the scrap merchants at Beighton where it was cut up in October 1966. *AEB5067*

70030

70000

70001

Opposite Top: No 70000 *Britannia* is seen at Halesworth as it heads south to London Liverpool Street with an express service from the east coast ports of Great Yarmouth and Lowestoft. Outside the goods shed, Class B1 4-6-0 No 61329 (built by the North British Locomotive Co [NBL] in June 1948) waits to take a freight service southward. No 70000 was allocated to Norwich Thorpe depot (32A) from January 1959 until moving to March in September 1961 and onto the London Midland Region at Willesden in March 1963. The image is not dated, however, No 70000 has received the modified arrangement of steps below the smokebox and sports the AWS protector plate, fitted during September 1959, beneath the buffer beam. *ICA BR149*

Opposite Bottom: No 70001 *Lord Hurcomb* on shed at Lowestoft whilst allocated to Norwich Thorpe. The locomotive would take the Lowestoft portion of a Liverpool Street service to Beccles where it would be joined by the Great Yarmouth portion for the run up to London south. On the northbound trip the train locomotive would take its portion back to Lowestoft. The locomotive depicts a stronger version of the step arrangement below the smokebox (compared with the image on page 29) and AWS protector plate, fitted during September 1959, beneath the buffer beam. The handrails on the smoke deflectors have been replaced by the LMR-style handhelds. *ICA BR90*

Above: No 70042 *Lord Roberts* at speed with an Up express near Ugley crossing, situated to the north of Elsenham, on 8th September 1956. When the line was built it crossed North Hall Lane at an acute angle resulting in the road approached being z-shaped. The locomotive sports heightened lamp irons above the buffers, and the first variation of the front step. *RCR7978*

70039

70041

Opposite Top: No 70039 *Sir Christopher Wren* approaches Cambridge on 27th April 1958 at the head of a Down express passenger service during the period when it was allocated to Stratford. The tracks alongside the line to the right were part of the Upper Yard Goods area. No 70039 was reallocated to Norwich in January 1959 and finally departed East Anglia for Immingham depot in December 1960 along with Nos 70040/1. The train consists of a mix of LNER and BR stock in the later BR maroon and the earlier 'blood & custard' liveries. *RCR11731*

Opposite Bottom: No 70041 *Sir John Moore* is seen on shed at Cambridge during 1953 having worked in from London Liverpool Street while allocated to Stratford. Transferred to Norwich, it stayed there for less than two years before its reallocation to Immingham that occurred at the end of 1960. The shed at Cambridge was opened by the Eastern Counties Railway in 1847 and enlarged by the Great Eastern in 1913. Subsequently enlarged again in 1932, it gained a mechanical coaling plant and a larger, 70ft, turntable. It closed on 18th June 1962 and was demolished.

Right: No 70038 *Robin Hood* pulls away from Cambridge on 26th May 1953 with the 6.45pm service to Liverpool Street, having brought in the portion from Norwich. Visible in the original image is a reversed train name-board on the centre buffer beam lamp iron, no doubt the crew were making sure it was returned to its 'home' depot of Stratford. The large buildings to the right were two of the station's Goods Sheds. At the time of the 1923 Grouping the station was served by the GE, Great Northern, London & North Western and Midland companies, each with their own facilities.

At the head of an Up express No 70042 *Lord Roberts* enters Cambridge station on 1st June 1958. For many years the station possessed a single main line platform some 514 yards (470m) in length – the third longest in the country. It had a scissors crossover in the middle to divide it into two, allowing trains from either direction to pass those already stopped there. No 70042 was allocated new to Stratford before moving to the LMR at Kentish Town in June 1958, only staying for a short period before relocating to Trafford Park. *RH21-5*

Later in the day (see page 30) the RCTS 'Great Eastern Commemorative Steam Rail Tour', headed by Class J15 No 65567, has reached Thetford. Following its visit to the former Norwich Victoria station, and then running into Thorpe, No 70003 *John Bunyan* was serviced before running light engine to Thetford to take over from No 65567. With the signals pulled off the 'Britannia' awaits the 'right away' from the guard for the trip back to London Liverpool Street. The shed staff had got the whitewash out, painting the vacuum and steam-heat pipes along with buffers and some of the smokebox door fittings.

No 70012 *John of Gaunt* is seen at Beccles on 29th May 1959 as it combines the through coaches from Yarmouth and Lowestoft into a single train bound for Liverpool Street. Beccles was the eastern end of the Waveney Valley line which was a cross-country route running between Tivetshall in Norfolk and Beccles in Suffolk. The line was authorised by the Waveney Valley Railway Act of 3rd July 1851 with the line opening in stages, firstly from Tivetshall to Harleston on 1st December 1855, then to Bungay on 2nd November 1860, and finally to Beccles. Allocated to Norwich at the time, No 70012 moved to March depot in September 1961 with transfer to the London Midland Region occurring in March 1963. *AS E98-6*

Chapter 2 - Southern 'Britannias'

Opposite Top: Delivered new to Cardiff Canton on 8th November 1952, No 70029 *Shooting Star* was the last of the batch to be delivered to the Western Region. It is seen reversing out of London Waterloo station on 21st May 1953 when temporarily shedded at Exmouth Junction during the period the Bulleid Pacifics were withdrawn with suspected axle flaws. Alongside is the first LMS main line diesel, No 10000, which arrived on the Southern Region with No 10001, to allow direct comparison to be made with Bulleid's own design of main line diesel – Nos 10201, 10202 and 10203. Nos 10000/1 returned to the LMR in the spring of 1955, taking the Southern's locomotives with them. *RCR4579*

Opposite Bottom: No 70023 *Venus* gains speed as it approaches Vauxhall on 19th May 1953 whilst acting as temporary cover for the side-lined 'Merchant Navy' class Pacifics. Allocated to Salisbury, this was one of the locomotive's first workings, no doubt the grapevine, at that time, was almost as quick as today's technology. The locomotive returned to Old Oak Common depot in June. *RCR4565*

Above: On Saturday 2nd June 1951 No 70009 *Alfred the Great* was exhibited at Eastbourne for the opening of the Conference of the International Railway Union, the event was open to the public and Standards, Nos 75000 and 73001, were on view alongside Southern Region 3rd rail electric No 20003, the Fell diesel-mechanical No 10100 and SR diesel shunter No 15227. Four days later No 70009 is seen at the head of the 'Bournemouth Belle' as it passes beneath the signal gantry that spanned the tracks at the London end of Clapham Junction. The SR, and its predecessors, used the head codes to denote the route rather than the type of service being operated. The three locomotives allocated to the Southern (Nos 70004/9/14) had additional lamp irons on the smoke deflector stays enabling the correct route code to be carried as seen here; Nos 70017 and 70028/29 also acquired them at a later date when covering for temporarily withdrawn 'Merchant Navies'. The 'Bournemouth Belle' was introduced on Sunday 5th July 1931 providing a Pullman Car service from London Waterloo to Bournemouth West. Reintroduced following World War 2 on 7th October 1947, the service would survive until the last day of steam on the Southern Region on 9th July 1967, although latterly hauled by Brush Type 4 diesel locomotives; No D1924 hauled the last train and is still operational on the main line (as No 47810) with Locomotive Services Ltd. On 10th May 1965 the gantry that supported the signal box, the roof can be seen above the locomotive's cab, suffered a partial collapse following the failure of a diagonal tension member that resulted in the box dropping 4ft. Due to the swift action by the signalling staff there were no casualties. *REV55A-2-3*

70004

70014

Opposite Top: No 70004 *William Shakespeare* is seen passing through Eastleigh with an Up special freight train containing bananas on 17th August 1966. By this date the locomotive was allocated to Stockport Edgeley (9B) and had come down south to work the Westbury-Basingstoke-London Waterloo leg of the 'A2 Commemorative Rail Tour' on the 14th; LNER 'A2' class No 60532 *Blue Peter* had worked the first leg from Waterloo to Westbury via Basingstoke, Salisbury and Exeter. The Southern Region had 'borrowed' the 'Britannia' for a few days before sending it home; by this date the locomotive has lost its nameplates, with the engine in plain green livery towing a lined tender. No 70004 entered service on 30th March 1951, and, initially allocated to Stratford, moved to the Southern Region's Stewarts Lane depot the following October. At the time of the photograph No 70004 carried the original fluted coupling rods on the rear-section. *PP1657*

Opposite Bottom: Following delivery to Norwich on 2nd June 1961 No 70014 *Iron Duke* was loaned, a couple of weeks later, to Eastleigh for trials on express services from London Waterloo. It is seen here at Bournemouth Central with a Bournemouth West to Waterloo via Sway express service as denoted by the head code carried. Ten weeks later the locomotive was allocated to Nine Elms before a permanent transfer to Stewarts Lane in October 1953.

Below: No 70014 *Iron Duke* is seen sporting the full 'Golden Arrow' regalia at Dover shed on 8th May 1955. The 'Arrer' and its French equivalent, the 'Fleche d'Or', was a luxury boat train introduced in the UK on 15th May 1929 (the French train was introduced in 1926) operated between London Victoria and Dover using the newly introduced TSS *Canterbury*, built by William & Denny Bros, Dumbarton (2,910 grt, 1928), for the ferry crossing. Post-war, *Canterbury* served on the Folkestone-Calais route, transferring to the Calais/Boulogne run in 1948, when it became the first English Channel ferry to be fitted with radar. Withdrawn from service, the ship was dismantled in August 1965. No 70014 was one of two locomotives allocated to the 'Golden Arrow' service and they had their outer lamp irons heightened to stop the oil lamps blowing out; they were cut down when the locomotives were reallocated to the London Midland Region.

How the mighty have fallen. No 70014 *Iron Duke*, badly in need of a clean, is seen with a Down service at Sydenham Hill on 18th August 1957. The bolts, and dirt shadow, of the arrow are clearly visible on the smoke deflectors. Records show that the locomotives allocated to the Southern Region generally ran less than 30,000 miles a year, this increased considerably once they were transferred away. *RCR11097*

No 70017 *Arrow* is seen passing through Earlsfield with the last leg of a Plymouth-London Waterloo service. The locomotive carries an Old Oak Common shed code, where it was allocated from June 1951 until transferred to Cardiff Canton in December 1956. It however had a month's 'holiday' on the Southern in May/June 1953 when covering for the temporarily withdrawn 'Merchant Navy' Pacifics when the class was being checked for axle flaws. The canopy 'chimneys' are those of Durnsford Road Power Station that provided electricity for the third-rail electric multiple units. No 70017 appears to have had only a single additional lamp iron fitted to the smoke deflector stays, to the driver's side; together with a mixed of coupling rods. *REV 74B-3-1*

No 70014 *Iron Duke* is seen at Hildenborough on 3*rd* August 1951 with the boat train service from London Victoria to Dover or Folkestone via Tonbridge and Ashford. The four-wheel vans hung onto the tender would contain passengers' luggage. Having 'officially' arrived at 'the Lane' in October 1951, the locomotive would stay until its transfer to the London Midland Region in July 1958. *REV57B-5-1*

One of two locomotives allocated to front line services on the Southern Region's Eastern Division was No 70004 *William Shakespeare*, seen sporting the full 'Golden Arrow' regalia at Dover shed on 8th August 1956. Unlike the other locomotive No 70014, it does not appear to have the heightened lamp irons at this date. It has been recorded that the Stewarts Lane shed master Richard Hardy, arranged for the flags to be washed on a regular basis to maintain appearances. No 70004 was transferred away from the Southern Region in July 1958, bound for the London Midland Region.

Chapter 3 - Unloved on the Western?

It was recorded in railway publications at the time that the 'Britannias' were not generally welcomed with open arms by the Western Region (see *The Book of the Britannia Pacifics*) whilst there was some of the 'not invented here syndrome', it was more likely the fact that the 13 locomotives were spread over four depots and the top link crews did not get used to them. Once all were allocated to Cardiff Canton they became more accepted. No 70026 *Polar Star* awaits departure time with the 3.55pm London Paddington-Fishguard Harbour service on 30th July 1955. Arriving at Cardiff Canton in October 1952, No 70026 was one of the least relocated of the class with only four sheds to its name. Ex-GWR large Prairie 2-6-2T No 6125 lurks in an adjacent platform. On Sunday 20th November 1955 No 70026 was working an excursion from Treherbert to London Paddington and became derailed at Milton, Berkshire, when passing from the main to loop line due to excessive speed. The locomotive and several coaches rolled down an embankment that exacerbated the severity of the accident resulting in 11 fatalities and 157 injuries. This was the first fatal accident on the Western Region of BR; the locomotive was not re-railed until 4th December and did not return to service until July 1956. At the subsequent enquiry claims were made about signal views being obstructed by the handrails on the smoke deflectors. This led to the handrails being removed and replaced by handholds on many locomotives.

Above: Following its introduction to traffic on 15th September 1952, and a period of running in, No 70025 *Western Star* was sent to the Rugby Testing Station for a period of six months before reaching its allocated depot of Cardiff Canton in May 1953. A couple of months later it is seen awaiting departure time at London Paddington with an express service to Pembroke Dock, basically in ex-works condition. No 70025 would depart South Wales for Aston, working light engine via Shrewsbury in September 1961. Alongside is GWR 'King' class 4-6-0 No 6005 *King George II* dating from July 1927. *J. Patterson*

Below: Locomotives working in-bound services to London Paddington did not have to visit Old Oak Common to be serviced as the GWR had a site at Ranelagh Road, which was located south of the running lines opposite Royal Oak station, enabling locomotives to be turned and serviced. Cardiff Canton-allocated No 70019 *Lightning* is seen on 12th March 1958 having the 'Capitals United Express' headboard placed on the top lamp iron – this must have been a bit of an effort for those of a short stature. The named train was introduced in 1956, linking London and Cardiff, running until 1963. Surviving into the diesel era Ranelagh Road saw less use following introduction of the HST units, closing in 1980. *RCR11480*

Above: New to Laira depot on 3rd August 1951 No 70021 *Morning Star* spent over five years allocated there before being reallocated to Cardiff Canton early in 1957. It is seen in charge of the 1.55pm Paddington-Pembroke Dock service having just passed under Westbourne Bridge on 12th March 1958. Despite being allocated to the WR, this was one of the few locomotives not to receive handholds on the smoke deflectors, retaining handrails to the end. *RCR11483*

Below: The 3.45pm London Paddington-Swansea service is seen passing under Ranelagh Bridge minutes after departing for Wales on 30th August 1958. Ranelagh Bridge servicing point is off to the right – No 70029 *Shooting Star* would have been attended to there before reversing into Paddington to work the service westward back to its home depot of Cardiff Canton. It still sports a single additional lamp iron on the driver's side smoke deflector stay as a memento of its period on the Southern Region in 1953. Along with its classmates allocated to the Western Region, No 70029 would depart for Aston on 10th September 1961. *RCR12679*

A35

Top: Doing what it says on the tin. No 70018 *Flying Dutchman* passes Tilehurst at speed at the head of the 8am Cheltenham-London Paddington service on 1st August 1959 during the period it was allocated to Cardiff Canton. No 70018 arrived at Old Oak Common when new in June 1951, staying there until December 1956 when it moved to Wales at Cardiff (Canton). The locomotive sports the modified front step arrangement, Western Region-style handholds on the smoke deflectors and oblong section coupling rods. *RCR14013*

Bottom: No 70028 *Royal Star* hauls the 'Red Dragon' past Didcot East junction on 25th July 1953, passing an inter-regional service incorporating Maunsell Open Third No S1287S in its consist. Hidden behind No 70028's train is Didcot depot, which was opened by the GWR in June 1932 – using the government's Development (Loans Guarantees and Grants) Act of 1929 – it replaced an earlier shed dating from July 1857. Closed at the end of Western Region steam on 5th April 1965, it is now the home of the Great Western Society's collection of locomotives and rolling stock. *REV78B-6-3*

Above: The 8am Cardiff-London Paddington service passes Highworth junction on 14th May 1955 behind No 70025 *Western Star*. This was where the branch to the town left the main line to the east of Swindon. A passenger service for workers at the factory was provided from 1941 to 1944, and December 1956 to June 1957; however, the branch had lost its regular passenger service on 9th May 1953. Final closure to goods traffic occurred on 6th August 1962. *RCR6102*

Opposite Top: Whilst in charge of a Weston-super-Mare-Paddington service No 70017 *Arrow* pauses at Swindon, the 'home' of the Great Western. The locomotive still carries the reporting number of the previous train it worked, the 09.05 Paddington-Bristol service. Swindon Works carried out maintenance to the WR-allocated 'Britannias'. No 70017's last visit here occurred between 3rd June and 7th October 1957 when it underwent a Light Casual overhaul. Transfer to the LMR occurred in July 1958 before the inevitable occurring at Carlisle Kingmoor on 1st October 1966. The locomotive returned to South Wales for scrapping at the Newport yard of J. Cashmore.

Opposite Bottom: No 70028 *Royal Star* awaits departure from Swindon on 28th October 1958. The more aesthetically pleasing style of handholds was probably a result of a visit to Crewe Works between 28th May and 8th October the same year; an additional horizontal handrail has been fitted in line with the running plate. The crew pose for the photographer whilst waiting for the right away from the guard. No 70028 left the Western Region on 10th September 1961 bound for Aston. *LN2045*

70028
ROYAL STAR
86C
SC

Above: No 70027 *Rising Star*, and a fellow class member, are seen outside Swindon Works. Introduced to service on 7th October 1952, and mainly allocated to Cardiff Canton in the 1950s – it had the almost mandatory loan to the Southern Region during May 1953 – the locomotive had several overhauls at the works between February 1953 and September 1959 before having its only General Overhaul at Doncaster between 15th May and 13th July 1961; moving shortly afterwards to Aston. Note the additional shields behind the sand box filler covers. *NS207666*

Left: No 70026 *Polar Star* heads the Up 'Red Dragon' service through Coalpit Heath on 20th September 1955, two years into its eight year stay at Cardiff Canton. It is recorded that No 70026 was 'stopped' at Swindon when it was transferred to the LMR in September 1961. It entered Crewe Works on 28th November for a Heavy Casual overhaul, so presumably the WR were not prepared to spend money on a locomotive it was soon to lose – it emerged on 4th January 1962, returning to Aston where it would remain until transferred to Holyhead in April 1964. *RCR6836*

Above: Schools out on Friday 30th July 1954 as smartly dressed children enter No 70024 *Vulcan* into numerous notebooks. The location is the London end of Bristol Temple Meads station with the locomotive about to depart with an Up stopping service. Allocated to Laira at the time, transfer away from the Western Region to the LMR's Aston depot took place in September 1961. Alongside is GWR 'Hall' class 4-6-0 No 6957 *Norcliffe Hall*, dating from March 1943, that saw 22½ years service, the 'Britannia' just over 16 years – both well short of their anticipated service life.

Below: With its *Lord Roberts* name plates and shed code plates removed, No 70042 is seen on shed at Bristol Barrow Road in July 1965 having worked in from Holyhead where it was allocated at the time; it was one of the class not to be fitted with the Automatic Warning System. Transfer to Carlisle Kingmoor occurred by the end of the year where it would be withdrawn on 13th May 1967. Behind No 70042 stands a pair of Hawksworth 0-6-0PTs, the nearest has had its smokebox number plate removed and 9405 painted on; it was withdrawn the month before the image was taken. The Midland Railway opened the depot here in 1873, surviving until closure on 20th November 1965.

Top: No 70015 *Apollo* heads the 1.50pm Up Newquay-Paddington express at Whiteball on 21st July 1957. Allocated to Cardiff Canton at the time - where most of the Western Region allocated locomotives congregated before being transferred to the LMR – No 70015 left for Trafford Park in July 1958. *RCR7845*

Bottom: No 70016 *Ariel* runs through Stoke Canon on 21st July 1956 with the 1.35pm Penzance-London Paddington service. The original station opened in 1860, however, the Exe Valley Railway was opened on 1st May 1885 from a junction to the south of the station. The station was relocated so that it could serve both lines from 2nd July 1894. New loop lines were added in 1932 enabling express services to overtake freight and secondary trains. Closure to passengers occurred on 13th June 1960, whilst goods traffic survived until 3rd May 1965. No 70016 still retains fluted coupling rods on the rear section and has the modified front step arrangement, acquired during a General Overhaul at Crewe between 18th April and 1st June 1956. *RCR7793*

Opposite Top: No 70023 *Venus* departs Exeter St Davids for points west. The tracks leading off the foot of the image are the route 'up the bank' to Exeter Central that served the Southern's line to London Waterloo. St Davids was where GWR and SR trains running 'Up' to London were travelling in opposite directions. Carrying a Cardiff Canton shed plate the crew has not replaced the reporting code, as 234 refers to the 3pm Liverpool-Cardiff service.

Opposite Bottom: No 70019 *Lightning* awaits departure from Teignmouth on 4th August 1955 with an Up express passenger service during its period allocated to Plymouth's Laira depot where it arrived from Newton Abbot in September 1951. It left Laira at the end of 1956 for Cardiff Canton where it would remain until transfer to the LMR at Carlisle Kingmoor in September 1961.

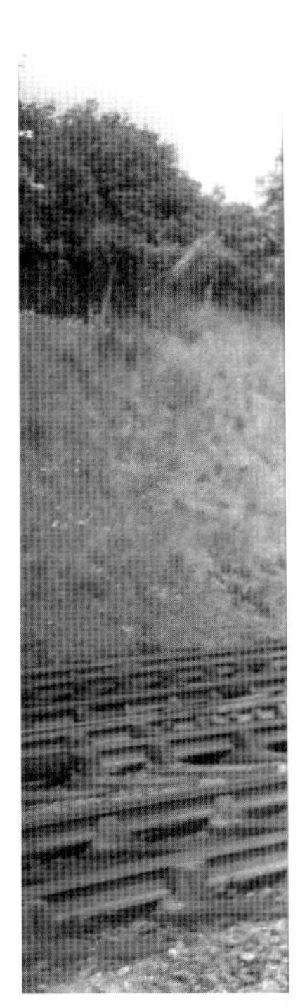

Above: Not the b
'Cornish Riviera'
Coronation perio
for main and bra
1931 under the D

Below: Having cr
'Cornish Riviera'
the timetables to
Automatic Train
LMR, initially at T
took place at Ca

Above: No
allocated tc
arriving at L
at Cardiff C
the locomo
steam on tl
1980s. *RC*

Below: No
west from i
to hide in tl
closed in A
1961 and r

No 70026 *Polar Star* with the modified smoke deflector hand holds clearly visible (the WR-design were given brass surrounds to avoid gripping the edge of the plate metal); the locomotive is seen at Cardiff Canton where it was allocated between November 1952 and September 1961 when it moved to Aston. Someone appears to have overloaded the tender with coal; hopefully it will not foul the loading gauge. A slightly decrepit No 70015 *Apollo* is doing its best to hide behind its cleaner rival. Transferred to the London Midland Region, No 70026 would be one of only two members of the class to be withdrawn from Stockport Edgeley, in this case on 14th January 1967. Cutting up took place at the Newport Yard of Cashmores in May 1967. *NS207700*

No 70027 *Rising Star* is seen departing Cardiff General with the 6.30am Swansea-London Paddington service on 1st June 1953, soon after its return from loan to the Southern Region; a Prairie is hiding behind the platform building. It left the Western Region, probably light engine via Shrewsbury, for Aston depot early in the morning on 10th September 1961 – where it would remain until allocated to Holyhead during May 1963. *RCR3883*

On 26th September 1959 No 70018 *Flying Dutchman* has charge of the 11.45am Manchester (London Road)-Plymouth service as it departs from Hereford; the crew have not displayed the train reporting number that should be 212. At this date the locomotive was allocated to Cardiff Canton. The vehicles on the left are ex-Great Western Railway 'Cordon' tank wagons used to transport gas to stations that were not connected to mains services – the gas was also used for catering vehicles and carriages not equipped with batteries for lighting. Transfer of No 70018 to Carlisle Canal took place on 10th September 1961. *WS515*

Above: No 70019 *Lightning* is seen on shed at Shrewsbury on 14th February 1960 carrying the train reporting number for the 8.50am Portsmouth-Birmingham service. The box attached to the underside of the bogie was part of the Western Region's Automatic Train Control system equipment that would ultimately be replaced by British Railways' Automatic Warning System. Transferred to the London Midland Region at Carlisle Kingmoor in September 1961, No 70019 spent the next five years shuttling round the region's depots until withdrawn from Carlisle Upperby on 12th March 1966. The West of Scotland Shipbuilding Co, Troon, dismantled it between that October and August 1967. *AS G90-3*

Left: No 70016 *Ariel* was the first member of the class to receive the 1956 totem in March 1956. As transfers were not available until the following year it must have been hand painted – maybe that is what the locomotive crew are looking at as No 70016 stands at Shrewsbury with the 4.10pm Swansea-Manchester service. Allocated to Cardiff Canton at the time of the photograph, the locomotive left the Western Region, along with the rest of its 'Britannia' allocation, in September 1961 when it transferred to Carlisle Canal. The locomotive has a mix of fluted and oblong coupling rods and has been retrofitted with the later style of sand box fillers. *H2484*

Chapter 4 - Eastern and North Eastern Travels

Above: No 70039 *Sir Christopher Wren* is seen approaching Hatfield station on 24th December 1960 at the head of a Cleethorpes (Grimsby)-King's Cross service, a few weeks after its arrival at Immingham depot where, along with its classmates, it operated express passenger and fast freight services. The locomotive was fitted with BR AWS equipment during a visit to Doncaster Works for a General Overhaul between 10th April and 10th June 1959. At one time there were branches from Hatfield to St Albans and Dunstable, the line off to the left leads to the goods sidings. *B. Wadey*

Below: No 70038 *Robin Hood* is seen approaching Brookmans Park station on 19th April 1962 at the head of the 4.12 Down Cleethorpes service whilst allocated to Immingham depot, and a few weeks after having a Light Casual overhaul at Doncaster in readiness for the summer season. It has received the additional running plate handrail by this time; its AWS was acquired during a works visit in the summer of 1959. The end of 1963 would see the locomotive transferred to Carlisle Upperby. *PP1311*

Above: Reallocated to Immingham in December 1960, No 70040 *Clive of India* switched its allegiance from Great Eastern to Great Northern rails, it is seen passing Peterborough's North Box at the head of a southbound express during 1961. It carries a 'non-standard' smokebox number plate, maybe the original had already been liberated by an enthusiast. Immingham depot made an effort to keep the locomotives smart, hence the whitened smokebox door straps. Transfer to London Midland metals occurred towards the end of 1963, and as with the majority of the class, it was withdrawn from Carlisle Kingmoor. Taken out of traffic on 15th April 1967, it was stored for several months prior to its demise in December the same year at Shettleston by McWilliams cutters. *NS207758*

Below: The Great Northern Railway established Doncaster railway works – always referred to as 'the Plant' – in 1853. Until 1867 it only undertook repairs and maintenance and replaced the previous works in Boston and Peterborough. Among the locomotives the works produced were the Stirling Singles, the Ivatt Atlantics and the Gresley Pacifics – including the world famous *Flying Scotsman*, the first locomotive to officially achieve 100mph and also haul the first non-stop train from London King's Cross to Edinburgh Waverley. One hundred years later the 'Plant' held its Centenary Exhibition at which No 70000 *Britannia* was displayed alongside 'home-built' motive power. Looking somewhat work worn, its footplate was open to visitors. Initially selected as part of the National Collection it was passed over in favour of No 70013 *Oliver Cromwell,* fortunately it survived to be privately preserved.

Above: No 70001 *Lord Hurcomb* visited Doncaster Works for seven weeks between 6th June and 24th July 1956 – the reason appears not to have been recorded – and again between 6th April and 25th May 1957 for a General Overhaul. It is pictured outside the works' Crimpsall shed carrying its 30A Stratford shed plate. Probably taken during the 1956 visit, the locomotive has 'don't move' chalked on the buffer, a red flag flying, with its connecting rod 'small end' resting on the ground. Compare its condition with that of the Standard Class 4 Mogul in front of it – 70 of the class were constructed at the works between December 1952 and October 1957. No 70001 would be withdrawn on 3rd October 1966 and recycled at Wishaw in January 1967. An interesting observation is that the 'Britannia' has straight lamp irons whilst the Class 4 has z-shaped ones to keep the head code disc/lamps clear of the running board. *NS207794*

Below: By now sporting a speedometer, fitted in September 1959, No 70006 *Robert Burns* is seen outside the works at Doncaster on 28th August 1960 having arrived two days earlier for a Non-Classified overhaul. Ex-works on 15th September, it returned to its home shed of Norwich Thorpe. The locomotive behind No 70006 is LNER Class B1 4-6-0 No 61202, built by the North British Locomotive Co in June 1947, and which had spent 11 days there for non-classified work. No 70006 was withdrawn from Carlisle Kingmoor on 20th May 1967 and stored there until October when it was consigned to J. McWilliams, Shettlestone, for scrap, being dismantled in November.

Above: The fireman of No 70053 *Moray Firth* has spotted the cameraman as the locomotive lifts an express service past Wortley junction just to the north of Leeds Holbeck station where the former Midland and North Eastern routes split. Introduced to traffic at Polmadie on 3rd September 1954, it would receive its nameplates on 2nd February 1955. Arrival at Leeds Holbeck occurred in October 1958, and then onto Crewe (North) in August 1962 – where it was allocated at the time of the image. By the time of the photograph the locomotive has been fitted with AWS, and an additional handrail in line with the running plate. *NS207631*

Below: New to traffic on 28th April 1951 No 70008 *Black Prince* entered traffic at Norwich, and by the date of the image sports the modified front step arrangement and is fitted with the AWS protection plate, the equipment being fitted in October 1959. The footplate crew of No 70008 has spotted the photographer as their charge heads a Class E freight service near Barlby junction, just outside Selby where lines from Hull, Market Weighton and York converged. The mineral wagons are acting as spacer vehicles between the locomotive and oil tankers that make up the bulk of the consist. The locomotive carries a March shed plate where it arrived in September 1961, so dating the image to that time frame as it moved to Carlisle Kingmoor in December 1963.

Right: Not obvious in the views of the RCTS rail tour of 31st March 1962 (pages 30 and 40), the AWS protector plate (the equipment was fitted in February 1960) beneath the buffer beam is clearly visible on No 70003 *John Bunyan* as it stands at York on 19th August 1961 with the 3.15pm Colchester service. At this time the locomotive was allocated to March where it had arrived in July 1961 following transfer from Norwich. In February 1963 it was reported that this was one of 13 class members to be in store at March depot as Class 37 diesels gradually took over the previously steam-hauled freight duties. By the end of the year No 70003 was shedded at Carlisle Kingmoor. *H2899*

Below: A favourite photographic haunt for holidaymakers was the turntable at Scarborough depot. No 70034 *Thomas Hardy* is seen on the manually powered 'table during 1961, having worked in from its home shed of March. The image can be dated to after 31st August as it was fitted with a speedometer during a General Overhaul at Doncaster between 5th July and 31st August – hence its general cleanliness. It has also gained a short horizontal handrail on the smoke deflectors in line with the running board and LMR-style handholds. Withdrawal would occur at Carlisle Kingmoor depot on 6th May 1967 with scrapping by McWilliams at Shettleston that October. *NS207732*

No 70037 *Hereward the Wake* and its express passenger train has just passed under Robin Hood bridge to the south of Lofthouse sometime in 1963, during the period it was allocated to Immingham. It was shopped at Crewe Works from 12th March-4 April 1963 and relocated to Carlisle Kingmoor, via Upperby, in January 1964. In October 1965 a coupling rod fractured and pierced the boiler, fortunately nobody was injured. Although it seems the locomotive never worked again, it was not condemned until 5th November 1966 with scrapping not taking place until February 1968. The author wonders if any photographers captured No 70038 passing under its namesake bridge? *NS207789*

Chapter 5 - Travelling around Scotland

Above: Glory days over, a somewhat work-stained No 70003 *John Bunyan* heads a southbound stopping passenger service through Beattock on the West Coast main line. Opened by the Caledonian Railway on 10th September 1847, the station closed on 3rd January 1972. Note that electrification south of Crewe has meant that the top head code bracket has been relocated to the side of the smokebox door reducing the chances of electrocution when putting the lamp onto the iron. Also noticeable, on the smokebox side of the smoke deflector, is the covering plate for the handholds – additional handrails have been added almost in-line with the top of the running boards. *NS207685*

Below: No 70053 with a Liverpool/Manchester-Glasgow service at Beattock on 4th December 1954. In the bay platform No 55232, an ex-Caledonian Railway Class 439 0-4-4T, awaits departure with the 1.55pm train to Moffat – this was the last day of passenger services on the 1.87-mile (3km) branch – freight services and occasional rail tours continued until 6th April 1964. When opened the spa town visitors had a service of 12 to 15 three-coach trains per day. In around 1926 this service was replaced by the 'Moffat Bus' or 'Puffer' steam railcar that worked the line until circa 1948. At the time of the image No 70053 was a couple of months away from receiving its *Moray Firth* nameplates. *WS2616*

Above: No 70047 entered traffic at Holyhead on 25th June 1954 and was the only BR Standard Pacific not to receive a name, it is seen at Beattock at the head of a tanker train. The locomotive would probably have worked out of Crewe (North) where it was shedded between November 1959 and August 1960, as it is fitted with AWS, received during a General Overhaul at Crewe between 29th October and 18th December 1959. Note that the leather 'bag' attached to the water crane has been tied to the column to prevent it blowing around; at some time between this and the image on page 73 the track has been re-laid with concrete sleepers. *SM020-10*

Opposite Top: No 70047 has 12 coaches, plus a van, and banker in tow as it takes the 10am Euston-Glasgow Central up Beattock bank near Greskine on 30th July 1960 whilst allocated to Crewe (North); a few days later the locomotive would be reallocated to Holyhead where it would remain until moved south to Willesden in June 1961. Four of the carriages carry train name boards on the brackets at roof level. *WS4846*

Opposite Bottom: No 70035 *Rudyard Kipling* was transferred to Carlisle Kingmoor in December 1963, having spent two periods at Norwich, along with stays at March and Immingham before arriving on the LMR (in December 1963) uniquely via a return to March depot in June 1963. It is seen passing Greskin, to the south of Beattock Summit, the following year. There was a signal box and loop here that enabled passenger services to overtake slower moving freight services. At some time the smoke deflector has received a 'hit', probably by the smokebox door locking handles. *NS204334A*

70035

No 70018 *Flying Dutchman* approaches Strawfrank Junction, Carstairs, on 31st July 1965 at the head of the 1.05pm Manchester-Glasgow service. The train will split at the station with Class 5MT No 45011 (alongside the train) waiting to take over the through carriages for Edinburgh Princes Street. At this time No 70018 was shedded at Crewe (North) and has lost its smokebox number and nameplates. The image was taken from the road bridge next to the three-storey signal box – the height of which enabled the signalman to see over the bridge towards oncoming trains from the south. Now known as Carstairs South junction, and the yards on the right a Permanent Way depot, the derelict track on the loading bay was still in situ in March 2017. *WS8226*

No 70002 *Geoffrey Chaucer* was transferred away from the Eastern Region on 1st December 1963 and moved to the London Midland Region, being allocated to Carlisle Kingmoor. It is seen here at Glasgow Polmadie depot having worked a service northwards. Although the image is not dated the end of steam is in sight as it has lost its nameplates, dating the image to sometime after July 1964. Alongside is Class 17 Bo-Bo No D8517, built by the Clayton Equipment Co it arrived at Polmadie on 29th June 1963; transfer to Kingmoor occurred in November 1967. However, the class was not successful and No D8517 was withdrawn 12th October 1968; outlasting No 70002 by less than two years as the 'Britannia' was withdrawn on 3rd September 1966.

The crew pose for posterity as No 70051 sits on Polmadie depot's turntable on 25th September 1954 a few weeks after entering traffic on 11th August; it would not receive its *Firth of Forth* nameplates until 11th January 1955. The Caledonian Railway opened the original depot here in September 1875; it was rebuilt by the LMS in 1925 and again by BR. It closed to steam on 1st May 1967 and saw further use as a diesel depot for a number of years. No 70051, along with Polmadie's other 'Britannias', Nos 70050 and 70052, was reallocated to Corkerhill in April 1962 – and all three arrived at Carlisle Kingmoor in January 1966. No 70051 was withdrawn on 16th December 1967, being sold to McWilliams for scrapping.

No 70039 *Sir Christopher Wren* waits for its 5.50pm departure time at Glasgow St Enoch with a Carlisle service on 5th May 1964, a few months after having been allocated to Carlisle Kingmoor where it was to remain until withdrawal on 23rd September 1967. Alongside is Polmadie-allocated Standard Class 4 2-6-4T No 80058, this was the final example built at Derby – the bulk of the class being built at Brighton – entering traffic on 8th January 1955, withdrawal came on 17th June 1966. *WS7411*

Above: The 6.40am Birmingham-Glasgow Central is seen passing Muirhouse Central junction on 15th July 1967 behind No 70028 *Royal Star*. Allocated to Carlisle Kingmoor, having arrived from Crewe (South) in September 1966, the locomotive would be withdrawn on 16th September 1967. Behind the locomotive is the island platform station of Pollockshields East that serves the Glasgow suburban services. No 70028 was one of a handful of locomotives not to be fitted with a speedometer drive. *WS9135*

Below: The 8pm Starlight Special from Glasgow St Enoch to London Marylebone is seen passing Shields Road on 13th July 1962 behind No 70052 *Firth of Tay*. Allocated new to Polmadie, where it arrived when new in August 1954 – it was not named until 6th January 1955 – it was transferred to Corkerhill in April 1962; its home depot at the time of the photograph. Already looking unloved, Shields Road station closed to passengers on 14th February 1966. *WS6221*

Above: Following transfer from the Southern Region to the LMR, No 70014 *Iron Duke* was initially allocated to Kentish Town. In December 1960 it was transferred to Newton Heath, Manchester, and is seen here leaving Glasgow Central at the head of the 12.25pm to Lockerbie on 4th March 1961. Transfer to Neasden occurred the following September, and it was one of the locomotives that retained the original smoke deflector handrails until withdrawal along with the bolts that once held the Golden Arrows in place. *WS5177*

Below: It is 14th September 1966 and a woebegone No 70010 stands on shed at Corkerhill having just been coaled; it was reported as having been in the paint shop at Crewe during May demonstrating how quickly appearance could deteriorate in daily use. Now allocated to Carlisle Kingmoor, the locomotive has lost its cast brass nameplates in 'favour' of painted versions, although in this case the Welsh spelling - *Owain Glyndwr* - has been adopted. In its final guise No 70010 now carries the AWS protector plate and speedometer drive and would remain in service for another year.

70050

35
70018

Opposite Top: No 70050 *Firth of Clyde* waits for departure time at Edinburgh Princes Street on 18th August 1955 with a Class B stopping passenger service. Allocated new to Polmadie on 4th August 1954, the locomotive spent almost eight years at the depot before a transfer to Corkerhill in April 1962. The 'L' shaped item on the buffer beam's central lamp iron is a route indicator, it enabled station staff to confirm the arriving train's destination enabling the correct packages to be put in the guard's van for onward transportation. The locomotive received the modified front step arrangement during a Light Casual overhaul at Crewe Works between 28th January and 9th March 1956.

Opposite Bottom: A smart No 70018 *Flying Dutchman* stands alongside Edinburgh Princes Street Gardens whilst allocated to Carlisle Canal, where it was shedded from September 1961 to May 1962 when it moved to Longsight. Following a final move to Carlisle Kingmoor in December 1966, the locomotive was withdrawn a few days later and consigned to Wishaw for disposal. Of note is that although LMR allocated, the locomotive retains its Western Region-style lamp irons; these would be changed by March 1963. *NS207702*

Above: No 70052 *Firth of Tay* is seen passing through Merchiston during 1962. On 21st January 1960 the driver of a Sleeper service from Glasgow to London heard a knocking sound on No 70052, near Settle, but could not identify the problem due to a snowstorm that night. He decided to precede to the next motive power depot, but before getting there, the locomotive's slide-bar failed and struck the tracks. The resultant damage derailed a freight train passing in the opposite direction with the wagons striking with the Sleeper train, killing five people and injuring nine. The locomotive was repaired at Crewe, re-entering service on 20th February. *NS207739*

No 70053 *Moray Firth's* stay in Scotland lasted just over four years before a move south to Leeds Holbeck in November 1958. Whilst allocated to Polmadie it is seen running light at Coltbridge junction on the outskirts of Edinburgh on 25th May 1956 when operating services between there and Glasgow. Having left Scotland, No 70053 spent time at Holyhead, Oxley and Banbury before it arrived at Carlisle Kingmoor in January 1966. It was withdrawn on 15th April 1967.

Top: No 70008 *Black Prince's* transfer to the LMR from the Eastern Region occurred by 7th December 1963 and it is seen at the head of a northbound express freight service at Larbert the following year. By this time the locomotive was allocated to Carlisle Kingmoor where it was to spend the rest of its career. A long way from home, the locomotive may have been 'borrowed' by either Glasgow Cockerhill or Polmadie depots as a replacement for a failed locomotive. This was one of the five class members to be withdrawn in January 1967. Larbert station building features a plaque commemorating the Quintinshill rail disaster in 1915, as it was from here that the ill-fated troop train involved in the accident originated. *NS207701*

Bottom: No 70041 *Sir John Moore* arrived at Carlisle Upperby from Immingham in December 1963 and is seen with the 9.25am Crewe-Perth service arriving at Larbert on 7th March. A member of the new order has been looped to enable the express service to overtake. The station was built by the Scottish Central Railway, opening on 1st March 1848. It is located on the main line from Glasgow Queen Street to Stirling and Perth near to the triangular junction with the line to Falkirk Grahamstown and Edinburgh Waverley. The SCR as first constructed linked the Edinburgh & Glasgow Railway main line at Greenhill with the Scottish Midland Junction Railway, with branches subsequently constructed to Polmont on the E&GR in 1850 and to Denny in 1858. The Polmont line remains in use today by services to and from Edinburgh, but the Denny line was closed to passengers by the LNER on 28th July 1930, with the Kilsyth branch following suit on 1st February 1935. *WS7308*

Above: Following its final transfer across Carlisle to Kingmoor, No 70041 *Sir John Moore* is seen at Perth at the head of the southbound 12.50 parcels service to Carlisle in July 1966. The station, opened on 22nd May 1848 as Perth General by the Scottish Central Railway, was designed by Sir William Tite, winning an architecture prize and is today a listed building. The locomotive had its last works visit between 24th March and 23rd April when it had a Heavy Casual repair at Crewe.

Below: On 30th May 1962 the 9.50am Euston-Perth service is seen at Gartsherrie South junction in charge of No 70020 *Mercury*. The junction was opened in 1848 connecting the Caledonian Railway's Coatbridge Central branch of the Garnkirk & Glasgow Railway (opened in 1843) to the North British Railway's Monkland-Kirkintilloch line. Having been allocated away from the Western Region in September 1961, 70020 was put on the books of Carlisle Kingmoor. The locomotive had a Heavy Casual overhaul at Crewe in April/May 1962 just before a move to Longsight took place in June. The final move to Carlisle Kingmoor took place in December 1966, just before its withdrawal on 21st January 1967. *WS6015*

Chapter 6 - Meandering around the LMR

Above: Just over four years after entering traffic, on 8th July 1954, No 70048 was named *The Territorial Army* 1908-1958 at Euston on 22nd July 1958 by the Duke of Norfolk; the nameplates were unusual in that they were red-backed at the time of the naming – it was advised that it was intended to transfer the name to a diesel in due course which did not happen. Cleaned to perfection, the locomotive had worked down to London from its home depot of Holyhead for the occasion and is seen shortly after the ceremony. *AS D91-5*

Below: No 70025 *Western Star* is seen on shed at Willesden during 1963 having worked Up to London from Crewe. It arrived there from Cardiff Canton via Aston in May 1963. The original depot at Willesden was opened by the LNWR in 1873; it was enlarged in 1898, although the new building was demolished in 1939. An additional square roundhouse had been opened and remained in use until 27th August 1965, the site subsequently being utilised as a Freightliner terminal. The locomotive sports Western Region-style hand holds on the smoke deflectors and AWS battery box and reservoir on the running plate that was fitted in December 1962.

Above: No 70004 *William Shakespeare* is seen entering Watford Junction with the 10.52am Up express service for Euston on 15th July 1961, a matter of weeks after having had a Heavy Intermediate overhaul at Crewe Works. The diamond on the signal post indicates to the driver that the area is track circuited (and if occupied indicated as such on a track diagram in the signal box) so that the crew need not contact the signalman if held at a red signal for longer than usual. The bolts, once used to hold the 'Arrows' to the deflectors, are still in place (see page 48). Alongside are examples of the original Watford electric (630V dc) carriages dating from 1914 that saw service until the 1960s. *H2737*

Opposite Top: No 70049 passes through Watford Junction on 30th March 1958; it would not receive its Solway Firth nameplates until the end of May 1960 – the last to be named, almost six years after entering traffic on 28th July 1954, whilst it was allocated to Newton Heath depot. With 17 sheds on its allocation record it was on Holyhead's books at the time of the image; it would be another year before it would be fitted with AWS during a General Overhaul at Crewe. Note the London Underground train on the right of the image as Watford Junction was the northern termini of the Bakerloo line. *AEB2926*

Right: Delivered new to Holyhead on 22nd June 1954, No 70046 ran over five years in service before receiving its Anzac nameplates during a short visit to Crewe on 10/11th September 1959. Anzac was an acronym for Australian and New Zealand Army Corps – a grouping of several divisions created early in World War 1 (1914-1918). It is seen here running through Watford Junction on 15th July 1961 at the head of a service bound for Manchester looking somewhat tired despite having a General Overhaul at Crewe at the beginning of the year when it was fitted with the AWS. Following the overhaul it returned to service at Longsight, staying until late summer 1961 when it was transferred to Willesden. *H2744*

Above: No 70010 *Owen Glendower* powers through Bletchley station with the 1M36 Down service from London Euston on 21st August 1964 whilst allocated to Willesden, where it arrived on 30th March 1963. Reallocation to Crewe (North) would take place in January 1965 following electrification of the main line to Crewe, Manchester and Liverpool. The gantries have been erected and await installation of overhead power lines and associated equipment. Withdrawal came on 23rd September 1967 and scrapping occurred at Shettleston in January 1968. *AS Q64-1*

Right: The final pair of the 1953 programme Nos 70043 and 70044, were the subject of braking trials. One of the intentions of the Modernisation Plan was the intention that all freight wagons would have power brakes; at Nationalisation some 600,000 coal and mineral wagons were fitted with hand brakes only, limiting the average speed to below 20mph. In 1950 the Railway Executive agreed on a trial to assess the relative merits of vacuum and air brakes for the operation of long and heavy mineral trains. Two hundred 16-ton coal wagons were fitted with continuous brakes – half with vacuum and half with air brakes. Trials took place mainly between Toton and Brent on the Midland main line – some 11,000 miles being run hauled by either No 70043 or 70044 that had been fitted with Westinghouse air brakes. One locomotive could handle trains of 70 empty wagons, but two were needed to double-head trains of 50 and 70 loaded vehicles. The trials determined that the vacuum brake was inadequate for trains of 70 loaded mineral wagons and either type of brake would require a means of increasing braking force. Either way it was determined that the vehicles themselves would require modification to buffing gear and bearings, however the conversion to air brakes was to be the way forward. The BTC asked the Regional General Managers for their comments, and all but one did not want to accept the operational problems that would exist during the conversion period. It took several decades for the vacuum brake to be eliminated from the main line network. With the air pumps located either side of the smoke box the locomotives did not carry nameplates until the deflectors were fitted. No 70043 is seen heading a Euston-Manchester express service at King's Langley on 16th October 1955 following its return to Longsight depot, naming as Lord Kitchener finally occurred during May 1957 having gained smoke deflectors to hang them on. Withdrawal took place at Crewe (South) on 7th August 1965.

No 70047 is seen at King's Langley in 1955 during its initial allocation to Holyhead depot, still with the original front step arrangement that would remain until March 1957 when it was revised during a Light Casual overhaul at Crewe Works between 28th January and 8th March 1957. The locomotive would move around the LMR including three periods allocated to Willesden depot before returning for a second stay at Holyhead between January 1964 and June 1965. *NS207818*

No 70024 *Vulcan* has charge of an Up fitted freight at Rugby on 4th November 1961; by this date the locomotive has lost its brass nameplates and cast iron smokebox plate in 'favour' of painted versions! At this time the locomotive was allocated to Aston depot, relocation to Rugby would come in October 1962. However, the footplate crews at Rugby did not appreciate their appearance and successfully campaigned for their replacement by Stanier Class 5s. It would be reallocated another 10 times before it was withdrawn on 30th December 1967 from Carlisle Kingmoor, meeting its end at the Killamarsh scrapyard of T. W. Wards in April 1968. In the background the Rugby works of Associated Electrical Industries can be seen. AEI was formed in 1928 by the merger of Metropolitan-Vickers and British Thomson-Houston. Of interest is that in 1937 Frank Whittle's Power Jet company built the world's first prototype jet engine at the BTH works in Rugby. *H. Gamble*

With coal piled high on the tender, No 70029 *Shooting Star* departs from Rugby Midland station with an Up express service during 1962 – nine years after its stint on the Southern Region it still carries an additional lamp iron on the driver's side smoke deflector support stay. At this date the locomotive was shedded at Aston depot where it had arrived on 10th September 1961. It would depart for Carlisle Kingmoor in October 1964 before moving to Upperby in November. Withdrawal would occur from Kingmoor on 21st October 1967 with scrapping at Shettleston the following March. *NS207790*

No 70047 has charge of 'The Irish Mail', the 1.25pm Holyhead-Euston service, at Rugby (Midland) on 14th July 1959. The locomotive would receive its AWS equipment during a General Overhaul at Crewe Works between 29th October and 18th December 1959. The steel bridge carries the Great Central line from London Marylebone to Manchester, virtually the entire GC route was closed in 1969, not managing to survive the 'Modernisation Plan' as traffic was transferred to former Midland lines. Had the line survived the cost of HS2 might have been avoided. *B. Wadey*

Above: No 70016 *Ariel* is seen near Great Bowden on 28th July 1962 as it heads the 12.25pm Manchester-St Pancras service whilst allocated to Longsight for a short period between June and September that year having arrived after a Heavy Casual overhaul at Crewe. It would be another year before the AWS equipment was fitted. As with the majority of the class, No 70016 arrived at Carlisle Kingmoor, in this case in October 1964; the locomotive would be withdrawn from traffic on 18th August 1967 and sold to McWilliams at Shettleston for scrap. *MM1885*

Below: Now allocated to Trafford Park, Manchester, (where it arrived in July 1958) No 70014 *Iron Duke* is at the head of the 12.50 London St Pancras-Manchester service at Kibworth on 21st August 1960. The Midland Railway opened the station here on 8th May 1857. As can be seen the lamp irons above the buffer beam have been cut back to their normal length following their heightening whilst on the Southern Region, although those on the smoke deflector stays remain. No 70014 would remain in traffic until 30th December 1967, when as with those remaining in general service it was withdrawn and, in this case, cut up at Inverkeithing in April 1968. *MM1299*

Above: The final member of the class to enter service was No 70054 that arrived at Polmadie depot on 13th September 1954 – receiving its *Dornoch Firth* nameplates on 7th February 1955. It is seen at Nuneaton with the Up 'Lakes Express' – running without the train nameboard - on 18th August 1964 whilst allocated to Crewe (North) shed. Transfer to Crewe (South) and Banbury occurred before its arrival at Carlisle Kingmoor in January 1966. It was withdrawn from there on 26th November the same year and was dismantled at Wishaw by the Motherwell Machinery & Scrap Co during May 1967. *AS Q53-2*

Below: No 70004 *William Shakespeare* departs from Trent with a variety of coaching stock in tow, suggesting that it might be a special working. The steam-heat pipe, to the left of the right-hand buffer, has been removed, and no shed plate is carried. In 1965 the locomotive paid a visit to Darlington Works, 16th December 1965 to 17th January 1966, to have front-end damage repaired; this was the first member of the class to visit the works, and the last to be 'shopped' before complete closure. No 70004 must have been in generally good condition as with the decline of steam No 70007 was withdrawn the same year. Withdrawn on 30th December 1967, No 70004 ended its days at the Inverkeithing yard of T. W. Wards during April 1968 – still carrying the original hand rails on the smoke deflectors together with bolts to hold the 'Golden Arrow' in place, and mix of coupling rods. *NS207686*

Right: No 70023 *Venus* stands in the platform at Crewe carrying a Class C head code denoting a 'parcels, fish, livestock, milk, fruit or perishables' service using passenger rated stock – the Royal Mail sacks on the platform a reminder of when the main method of transporting post around the country was by rail. The locomotive was allocated to Crewe (North) for a year from September 1963 to September 1964, dating the image to that period – it has lost its SC (self cleaning) plate fitted behind the shed plate. Note that the locomotive still carries the additional lamp irons to carry the route code when used on the Southern Region in 1953, over ten years before this image. *NS207746*

Below: On a dull 8th March 1965 No 70027 *Rising Star* heads an Up local service at Crewe. The overhead line electrification has been erected and the end of the 'age of steam' is within sight on the London Midland Region, with electric traction from London to Crewe and diesel haulage northwards. The locomotive was allocated at Crewe (North) from January 1965 before moving to the South shed in May following the closure of its former home. The end for No 70027 occurred on 1st July 1967 and, following a period in store, it was scrapped at Wishaw by the Motherwell, Machinery & Scrap Co the following November. *AS R58-2*

No 70031 *Byron* was the first true LMR 'Britannia' in that it was never allocated away from the region, arriving at Holyhead on 29th November 1952. It is seen at Crewe station with the 8.30am Euston-Manchester service on 31st May 1956. At this time the locomotive was allocated to Longsight depot where it would remain until transferred to Trafford Park in April 1960. Alongside No 70031, LMS 'Princess Royal' class 4-6-2 No 46209 *Princess Beatrice* waits to take over a northbound service, whilst allocated to the nearby Crewe (North) shed where No 70031 would be allocated to in December 1964.

No 70049 runs past Crewe North Junction signal box on 28th August 1954 three months after delivery from the nearby works, it has yet to have its '6J' - Holyhead - shed plate fitted. It shows perfectly the 'ex-works' condition that the later locomotives would enter traffic looking like. No 70049 would not receive its Solway Firth nameplates until late May 1960 soon after a Light Casual overhaul at Crewe Works, the last of the class to receive a name. It is noted on the locomotive record card that the intention was to name the locomotive Sir Henry Fowler.

Brand new from Crewe Works, on 15th September 1952, No 70025 *Western Star* is running in before being consigned to the Rugby Testing Station where it was to spend over four months (11th October 1952 to 27th February 1953) undergoing controlled trials; the tender has yet to be fitted with the step on the sloped top edge. In spring 1966 No 70025 spent a couple of months allocated to Llandudno for service along the North Wales coast before a transfer to Crewe (South) in April. It moved along with most of its classmates to Carlisle Kingmoor, arriving in September 1966, surviving until 23rd December 1967; meeting its demise in Campbell's yard at Airdrie the following January after a short period in store. *NS207625*

Hidden behind its own camouflage smoke, the crew of No 70015 *Apollo* proceed cautiously as the 9.30am departs Leicester Central with a local service to Nottingham Victoria on 4th November 1961. This was part of the former Great Central Railway route that opened in 1898 and closed in 1969. Today part of the route from north of Leicester to Loughborough operates as the heritage Great Central Railway with plans to extend to Ruddington (to the south of Nottingham) once fund raising to bridge a gap to the north of Loughborough station is in place. Allocated to Neasden at the time, No 70015 would see use at six depots before withdrawal from Carlisle Kingmoor on 5th August 1967. *MM1674*

On 24th April 1965 the Locomotive Club of Great Britain ran its 'Notts and Lincs Rail Tour', a trip involving No 70052 *Firth of Tay*, LNER Class B16 4-6-0 No 61406, LMS Class 2-6-0 No 43108 and LMS Class 4F No 44401. The 'Britannia', by now sporting plain green livery, ran from London St Pancras to Nottingham Midland where it is seen waiting to take the return trip back to London. The nameplate background appears to have been painted in light blue – perhaps as homage to its former home in Scotland. In September 1965 this was one of eight locomotives to be allocated to the former GWR Banbury shed, although by now it was in LMR territory, all left in January 1966 bound for Carlisle Kingmoor; withdrawal came on 1st April 1967. *B. Waddy*

On Sunday 3rd April 1966 No 70012, by now minus its *John of Gaunt* nameplates, hauled the Epsom Railway Society's 'Midland Enterprise' special from Derby to Crewe where it is seen soon after arrival. With no Health & Safety concerns, enthusiasts try to get the best photographs. The train ran from London St Pancras, via Derby and Crewe, before returning to London Paddington. At this time the locomotive was allocated to Llandudno Junction, its stay here was short as it arrived week ending 26th February before a move in April to Crewe (South) followed by a final relocation to Carlisle Kingmoor in August, from where it was withdrawn on 30th December 1967. *AEB7100*

The 'Irish Mail' is seen at Crewe on 31st July 1954 in charge of No 70046, a little over a month from when the locomotive entered traffic, and it would be another five years before the locomotive was named. The locomotive was to be shuttled around the LMR, with three stays at Holyhead and two at Kingmoor before its short career ended there on 8th July 1967; meeting its demise at the hands of Campbell's in Airdrie during January 1968.

With the end of steam traction firmly in sight, the Severn Valley Railway Society and Manchester Rail Travel Society ran their 'Farewell to BR Steam' excursion on 28th July 1968, an out and back tour from Birmingham New Street to Stockport Edgeley. No 70013, complete with hand painted Oliver Cromwell on the deflectors, supplied the motive power for the Manchester Victoria-Carnforth leg. Of the six steam locomotives used for various parts of the tour, three survive in preservation. No 70013 is seen passing Boar's Head Junction signal box to the north of Wigan on the North Union Railway (later LNWR) line to Preston. Three weeks later steam on BR's standard gauge lines came to an end. The station at Boar's Head opened on 31st October 1838, closing on 31st January 1949. *NS207623*

Above: New to traffic at Holyhead on 10th December 1952, No 70032 moved to Longsight in January 1953. The shed's cleaners put in the elbow grease as Tennyson is cleaned to perfection on 15th March 1953 for its naming ceremony two days later. Its appearance is in stark contrast to the work-weary LMS 'Jubilee' 4-6-0 No 45680 Camperdown and 'WD' 2-8-0 that has had its motion removed. The 'Britannias' allocated to Longsight were used on class 7 duties alongside the rebuilt 'Royal Scots'. No 70032 moved across the city to Trafford Park early in 1960.

Below: With 12 carriages in tow, No 70049 *Solway Firth* is seen on the bank at Tebay during 1960 following its naming in May. Allocated to Newton Heath, where it had arrived from Crewe (North) in January 1960, No 70049 would remain there before departing for Neasden in early 1961. The locomotive served at a further 10 depots before a final arrival at Carlisle Kingmoor in December 1966, from where it was withdrawn on 9th December 1967. *NS209136*

No 70050 is seen awaiting departure from Preston on 16th September 1954 barely six weeks after introduction to traffic at Polmadie, the locomotive received its *Firth of Clyde* nameplates on 19th January 1955. Alongside is No 42432, a Stanier-designed 2-6-4T; dating from March 1936 it was in traffic for over 29 years, the 'Britannia' served for less than 12. The water column, to the right of No 70050, has its reference number on a cast plate and a painted note as to which way to turn the handle off. No 70050 was withdrawn from Carlisle Kingmoor on 6th August 1966, being cut up by the end of the year in the Airdrie yard of G. H. Campbell where almost 200 steam locomotives were cut up.

70011

1X75
THE GRANITE CITY

Opposite Top: No 70011 was transferred to the former LNWR depot of Carlisle Upperby in February 1965, before a final move to the nearby ex-Caledonian Railway's Kingmoor shed to the north of the city in December 1966. Having lost its *Hotspur* nameplates, No 70011 is illustrated at Preston on 19th May 1967 at the head of an express service – the AWS and speedometer had been fitted during the spring of 1960. This was one of a number of the earlier locomotives not to receive the extended sandbox fillers on the running plates. No 70011 would be withdrawn on 23rd December 1967 and scrapped at Shettleston in April 1968.

Opposite Bottom: On Saturday 3rd September 1966 the South & West Railway Society ran its 'Granite City' special from London Euston to Aberdeen, returning to London King's Cross (behind a Class 47 diesel) on the Sunday. No 70032 *Tennyson* took the train from Preston, where it is seen before departure, to Carlisle. It is interesting to note that the Society's headboard was designed for use on the traditional top headlamp bracket, not the 'side-mounted' version on 'Britannias' by this date due to overhead electrification. *NS203858*

Above: On 24th August 1963 No 70044 *Earl Haig* runs into Preston station with a southbound service whilst allocated to Crewe (North). Along with No 70043 this locomotive was involved in the air-brake trials before being returned to the standard format. Nos 70043/44 were originally destined for delivery to the Great Eastern, but the air-brake experiment meant that Longsight's Nos 70030/34 went in their place. Having been returned to standard, No 70044 received its nameplates on 16th March 1957, four months before its trials mate. It was withdrawn from Stockport (Edgeley) depot on 21st May 1966.

PRESTON
1K76

70003

Opposite Top: Holyhead-allocated No 70045 received its *Lord Rowallan* nameplates on 16th July 1957 and is seen here on the 27th as it waits in a bay platform at Preston to take over the Up 'Lakes Express' on its journey south. New to traffic on 16th June 1954, this was the first of the last 10 of the class to be fitted with a BR1D curved top tender and speedometer when built, along with both regulator rodding brackets. The locomotive was fitted with AWS during a Light Casual overhaul at Crewe Works between 1st and 27th October 1959. The locomotive received LMS-style oval headed buffers in 1966 following collision damage. As with the majority of the class, a final transfer to Carlisle Kingmoor occurred, in December 1965, with withdrawal on 30th December 1967. The 'Lakes Express', running from London Euston to Windermere, Keswick and Workington was revived following World War 2 and lasted until 1965.

Opposite Bottom: No 70003 minus its *John Bunyan* nameplates, standing alongside the coaling stage at Carnforth depot on 8th July 1966. The data chalked on the smokebox door - 1M38 - is a train reporting number: the 1 indicates the class of train, the M the destination area (in this case the Midland), and 38 the individual train. No 70003 would be withdrawn from Carlisle Kingmoor on 25th March 1967, and cut up by the end of the year at Campbell's Airdrie yard. Carnforth depot was rebuilt by the LMS in 1944, with the new facilities including a cast concrete mechanical coaling tower and 70ft turntable; closed with the end of steam on BR it is today, the home of West Coast Railways – operators of steam-operated services on the main line.

Above: The 2pm Glasgow Central-Liverpool/Manchester service storms out of Carlisle Citadel on 12th August 1967 behind No 70032, with not a clue (apart from having lost its Tennyson nameplates) that it was seven weeks away from withdrawal. Perhaps the news had got around as there are a number of enthusiasts leaning out of the carriage windows. It is recorded that having lost its cast nameplates it was 'renamed' Lord Tennyson (in paint) for a period during 1965/66. No 70032 entered traffic with a BR1 tender, but ran with a 'curved top' BR1D for most of 1967 as seen here. *WS9163*

70022
45293

Opposite Top: No 70022 *Tornado* arrived at Carlisle Kingmoor, from Cardiff Canton, in September 1961, and is seen alongside the platform at Carlisle station a few days later on the 18th. Having been released from its inbound service, No 70022 will head to the sheds whilst Stanier Class 5MT No 45293 stands on one of the centre roads waiting to take the service onwards. No 70022 would move around various LMR sheds before returning to Carlisle Upperby in November 1964, a move across town just over two years later would see it arrive at its final depot.

Opposite Bottom: No 70041 *Sir John Moore* has charge of the 9.25am Crewe-Perth service seen here passing Port Carlisle junction on 8th May 1965. This was the junction between the former Caledonian and North British company lines to the north of Carlisle Citadel station as it was known then. By this date No 70041 has lost its nameplates and would be withdrawn on 15th April 1967 and cut up by McWilliams at Shettleston in October the same year. *WS8018*

Right: The 2pm Glasgow Central to Liverpool and Manchester service leaves from platform 4 at Carlisle Citadel on 22nd July 1967 behind No 70038 *Robin Hood*, which has attracted the attention of a number of enthusiasts witnessing the decline of steam traction. The locomotive's cast nameplates have been removed, only to be replaced by hand-painted versions. Withdrawn only a few weeks later on 12th August, the locomotive would be a pile of scrap metal by February 1968. *WS9143*

Above: New to traffic on 13th December 1952, No 70033 simmers outside the shed at Carlisle Kingmoor, the locomotive has lost its *Charles Dickens* nameplates but, unlike many of the class, retains the hand rails on the smoke deflectors; the AWS battery box on the running plate is clearly visible. The pipework on the ground alongside the locomotive is a pile of superheater elements, presumably salvaged from locomotives sent for scrap. No 70033 entered traffic at Holyhead and, after doing the usual round of LMR depots, arrived at Kingmoor in June 1965. Withdrawal occurred from there on 15th July 1967, joining the list of those scrapped by Campbells at Airdrie. *SM124*

Opposite Top: A filthy No 70005, minus its *John Milton* nameplates, stands on shed at Kingmoor towards the end of steam; the locomotive had been noted in the Erecting Shop at Crewe Works, on 16th January 1966, with fellow classmates Nos 70011/40/45 – in its case a Light Intermediate overhaul was taking place. Standing behind in the shadows is a 'Clan' class Pacific – either 72006 or 72008, both of which survived until the spring of 1966. No 70005 would survive until withdrawn on 29th July 1967, being broken up by Campbells, Airdrie, in January the following year.

Opposite Bottom: Having received the Automatic Warning System during a Light Intermediate overhaul at Crewe between 12th October and 12th November 1959, No 70048 *The Territorial Army* 1908-1958 followed the usual style of moving around various LMR sheds before arriving at Carlisle for its final few years of service. The locomotive was initially allocated to Kingmoor in October 1964 then crossed the town to Upperby in November 1964, where it is seen on shed, before returning to Kingmoor shed in December 1966.

70005

70048

1Z35
1Z35
70031

Opposite Top: No 70031 minus its *Byron* nameplates, although still with handrails on the smoke deflectors, runs over the troughs at Dillicar. The troughs enabled a locomotive to take water whilst on the move. Although designed and installed for steam locomotives, they were also used by diesel locomotives to replenish the water supply for their steam heating boilers. Troughs were laid between the rails and were typically a little over a quarter mile long; a scoop on the locomotive was lowered into them where the train's movement caused sufficient pressure to force the water up and into the locomotive's tank. The smoke box has a reporting number chalked on it, twice, unfortunately the photographer did not record the actual date or service. *NS207617*

Opposite Bottom: No 70035 *Rudyard Kipling* is here at Shap Wells during 1964, a popular spot for photographers during steam's later years. By now allocated to Carlisle Kingmoor the locomotive, albeit in filthy condition, would survive in traffic for another three years; being noted in the erecting shop at Crewe Works on 27th June 1965 in the company of No 70054. It would be withdrawn, along with 13 other members of the class, in December 1967 – leaving No 70013 to soldier on to the end of steam. T. W. Wards at Inverkeithing would scrap it in April 1968. *NS203879B*

Above: A low-level shot of No 70047 at Penrith in 1960 gives the locomotive a powerful appearance. It would be withdrawn from Carlisle Kingmoor depot on 19th July 1967 and cut up at Airdrie by Campbells during December. The AWS protector below the buffer beam can be clearly seen; there is no smokebox allocation plate in place so the picture may have been taken around the time of its transfer from Crewe (North) to Holyhead that took place in August 1960. *NS209201*

Above: No 70028 *Royal Star* poses on the turntable at Skipton on 16th March 1967. Withdrawal would occur six months later at Carlisle Kingmoor, where it arrived a year earlier from Crewe (South). McWilliams at Shettleston scrapped it in February 1968. Unlike a number of locomotives it appears to have no covers for the hand holds on the inner side of the smoke deflectors. The shed at Skipton was rebuilt by the LMR in 1951, complete with a turntable in the shed yard; the depot closed on 3rd April 1967. The shed building was demolished during 2021 to make way for a new waste services building.

Below: On 26th December 1952 No 70031 *Byron* passes Gledholt junction signal box on the former Midland Railway, after passing through a tunnel it will connect with the Lancashire & Yorkshire line at Spring Wood junction for the final run into Huddersfield whilst allocated to Holyhead. Transferred to Longsight in January 1953, it would remain there until April 1960 when it moved to Trafford Park. As with many locomotives, withdrawal came at Carlisle Kingmoor on 11th November 1967 and, after a short period of storage, was cut up four months later by McWilliams at Shettleston.

No 70048 *The Territorial Army* 1908-1958 passes Llandudno Junction during August 1958 at the head of the 'Irish Mail'. The named train operated from London Euston via the West Coast and North Wales Coast lines to Holyhead from 1948 until 2002, connecting with ferry services to Dublin. The locomotive was withdrawn from Kingmoor on 6th May 1967, with less than 13 years service, to be scrapped by McWilliams at Shettleston in October.

Chapter 7 - Untimely Demise

No 70022 stands 'dead' at Carlisle Kingmoor following its withdrawal on 23rd December 1967. The crank on the trailing axle provided the drive for the speedometer. The speedos were not fitted to the first 45 locomotives when new but the majority of them received the equipment starting in December 1959. Following a period in store at Kingmoor, the end came at T. W. Ward's Inverkeithing scrapyard in March 1968.

Locomotives Illustrated